Hearing the Word of God

Hearing the Word of God

Reflections on the Sunday Readings
Year C

John R. Donahue, S.J.

LITURGICAL PRESS
Collegeville, Minnesota

www.litpress.org

Year B: ISBN 0-8146-2783-8
Year C: ISBN 0-8146-2784-6

1	2	3	4	5	6	7	8	9

Library of Congress Cataloging-in-Publication Data

Donahue, John R.
    Hearing the Word of God : reflections on the Sunday readings : year B / John R. Donahue.
       p. cm.
    Includes bibliographical references.
    ISBN 0-8146-2783-8 (alk. paper)
      1. Church year meditations. 2. Bible—Meditations. 3. Catholic Church—Prayer-books and devotions—English.   I. Title.

BX2170.C55 D615 2002
242'.3—dc21

2002067634

Contents

Calendar for 2003–2004

Introduction

"Hearing the Word" was selected as the title for these reflections on the three-year cycle of readings, since it evokes the first sentence of the Dogmatic Constitution on Divine Revelation from the Second Vatican Council: "Hearing the Word of God with reverence and proclaiming it with faith . . ." This decree reemphasized the primacy of Scripture in preaching, teaching, and Church life. Later in the same document, the council stated:

> The Tradition that comes from the apostles makes progress in the Church, with the help of the Holy Spirit. There is a growth in insight into the realities and words that are being passed on. This comes about in various ways. It comes through the contemplation and study of believers who ponder these things in their hearts (cf. Luke 2:19, 51). It comes from the intimate sense of spiritual realities which they experience. And it comes from the preaching of those who have received, along with their right of succession in the episcopate, the sure charism of truth. Thus, as the centuries go by, the Church is always advancing towards the plenitude of divine truth, until eventually the words of God are fulfilled in her (no. 8).

Preaching, teaching, study, religious experience—all are necessary to plumb the riches of Scripture. This is the world of the whole Church, and the religious experience of believers is a source of this development.

These reflections, which first appeared in the national Jesuit weekly *America* from November 2000 to Advent 2001 are an attempt not only to hear the Word of God in Scripture but to hear the hearers of the Word, suggesting ways that the Sunday readings might continue to nurture faith and life. Inevitably, then, they reflect at times the time in which they were first written. The world was shocked by the tragedy of September 11, 2001, and its continuing aftermath. Naturally these events influenced some of the Sunday reflections. Still, sadly, it seems that senseless violence will overshadow our pilgrim journey well into this century, so hopefully reflections on the Scripture from that period will take root in other situations.

I want to express special gratitude to many readers who have written me with comments on my reflections—both critical and supportive. I regret that I was unable to respond to them. I would like also to thank Fr. Thomas Reese, S.J., the editor of *America*, who invited me to do the original columns. No gratitude is really adequate for the work of Fr. Robert Collins, S.J., the managing editor of *America*, who shepherded the work toward publication. I am also most appreciative of the work of Mark Twomey, editorial director of the Liturgical Press and the editorial staff there, which produces such a visually attractive volume.

In talking to many groups of priests, religious, and laypeople over the years, I have suggested that we should always find the good news in a particular Sunday gospel in the context of a whole Gospel. There is a rhythm of interpretation where the richness of a particular passage comes from the theology of the whole Gospel, while simultaneously shaping its theology. Concretely put, to preach or pray over any given section of Luke (Cycle C), a person should be immersed in the theology and literary quality of the whole Gospel. I have included a short appendix of works that will hopefully contribute to enriched engagement with Luke and lead readers to treasure in their hearts those deep spiritual realities they experience.

JOHN R. DONAHUE, S.J.

Raymond E. Brown
Distinguished Professor of New Testament Studies
St. Mary's Seminary and University, Baltimore, Maryland

First Sunday of Advent

Readings: Jer 33:14-16; Ps 25; 1 Thess 3:12–4:2; Luke 21:25-28, 34-36

> **"You are God my savior,**
> **and for you I wait all the day" (Ps 25:5).**

THE BEGINNING OF THE END

In a recent issue of *Natural History*, the astrophysicist Neil de Grasse Tyson, director of the Hayden Planetarium, wrote: "If the events that span the fifteen billion year timeline of the universe were laid along the length of a football field, then all of human history would span the thickness of a blade of grass in the end zone. . . . the denouement is the still uncertain fate of the universe." As a new liturgical cycle begins, the First Sunday of Advent again reminds us that our lives are caught up in a cosmic drama and that history will end with the return of Christ and the redemption of humanity.

While the Bible does not teach science and the diverse images of the end–time should not be interpreted literally, Luke and Paul urge that Christians live not only looking back to what Christ has done for them, but also with an eye toward the future. Despite the emphasis throughout his Gospel on the joyful benefits of God manifest in Jesus, in this apocalyptic section Luke's Jesus is more concerned about negative behavior: carousing, drunkenness, concern for the anxieties of daily life. Jesus here virtually paraphrases the Lord's Prayer in asking for God's protection in the time of trial. Paul, who when writing 1 Thessalonians expected Jesus to return in his lifetime, is more positive. He prays that his community, while waiting, may abound in love "for one another and for all," "strengthen [their] hearts," and "conduct yourselves to please God."

All of us know how a coming major event, such as a wedding, a graduation, a visit from friends, or an examination, can shape our lives. These readings and Advent's stress on the Second Coming, as we prepare to celebrate the first coming of Jesus in history, remind us that

Christians should shape their faith in terms of hopes as well as memories. Jeremiah promises a time when Jerusalem will be secure and the people will call "the LORD our justice." In a world where peace and justice seem so impossible to achieve, Advent tells us that even in the face of suffering and death we must never let hope die, and that by expressing our hope in love for one another, we will create a portion of the promised future.

PRAYING WITH SCRIPTURE

- Express in prayer your deepest hopes about the ways in which Christ may come into your life.

- Look at the stars and think of the magnitude and mystery of God's creative love.

- Pray over how you may "strengthen [the] hearts" of loved ones during this season.

Second Sunday of Advent

Readings: Bar 5:1-9; Ps 126; Phil 1:4-6, 8-11; Luke 3:1-6

> **"The LORD has done great things for us;
> we are are glad indeed" (Ps 126:3).**

MAN OF THE YEAR

The readings today throb with a sense of joyful expectation. The prophet Baruch echoes a hope for release from exile and oppression by portraying "Lady Jerusalem" as a priest who takes off the robes of mourning and puts on the cloak of God's justice and the miter that displays the glory of God's name. God will bring the people back to Jerusalem and will lead Israel in joy. Psalm 126 is a joyous song of ascent, sung by pilgrims on their way to Jerusalem; and in writing to his favorite community at Philippi, Paul prays that they be filled with joy as they await the day of Christ.

The Advent gospels for all three Lectionary cycles highlight John the Baptist and Mary as figures of joyful expectation of the coming of Christ, yet each has its own particular slant. After the parallel stories of the conception and birth of John and Jesus, and the presentation of Jesus in the Temple, Luke adds a second and solemn introduction to the ministry of Jesus. Following the style of ancient historians, he dates the appearance of John according to the ruling powers. It is the fifteenth year of Tiberius (A.D. 28), Augustus's successor, who was strongly anti-Jewish. Luke names Pontius Pilate, who was governor of Judea; three client kings, who served at Rome's pleasure; and the high priests Annas and his son-in-law Caiaphas (who was the high priest in office, while Annas remained the power behind the office). Luke's readers would have known of the brutality of the Roman rulers and that Jesus was crucified under these same powers.

The rhythm of these cadences prepares the reader for some earth-shaking imperial event, only to be caught up short by the simple statement that "the word of God came to John the son of Zechariah in the

3

desert." Luke shifts from the style of royal chronicle to the call of a prophet. The coming of the word of God is a standard formula for a prophetic call, in this case to John as he prepares the way for Jesus, just as this word came to Mary at the Annunciation. John emerges "in the desert," the wilderness, which evokes Israel's journey from Egyptian slavery to freedom and the place where the covenant was inaugurated. He preaches and proclaims a ceremony of immersion, which is to symbolize interior repentance leading to forgiveness.

But for Luke, who puts the extended quotation of Isaiah 40:3-5 on the lips of John, John's more important task is to prepare the way of (or for) the Lord so that "all flesh shall see the salvation of God." Having begun the section with a list of rulers who did not bring wholeness or salvation, Luke ends with the expectation of a true Lord who can bring these about. Mary's prophecy begins to unfold: rulers will be thrown down from their thrones, while the lowly are exalted.

Luke also stresses that both John and Jesus are immersed in a particular people's history in a world-historical context. Luke's readers are to find God in history—first in the history of Jesus and then, in the Acts of the Apostles, in the history of the expanding Church.

The Church today faces a similar challenge as it prepares every year for the coming of Christ. Luke's perspective that "all flesh" shall see God's salvation is captured by the memorable beginning of the Second Vatican Council's Pastoral Constitution on the Church in the Modern World: "The joys and hopes, the grief and the anguish of the people of our time, especially of those who are poor or afflicted, are the joys and hopes, the grief and anguish of the followers of Christ as well. Nothing that is genuinely human fails to find an echo in their hearts" (no. 1). The document goes on to say that the Church must read the signs of the times and "be aware of and understand the aspirations, the yearnings, and the often dramatic features of the world in which we live" (no. 4).

Today, when the ruling powers, whether political figures or multinational corporations, seem as impervious to the Gospel as Luke's monarchs, the season of expectation can still be a season of prayer that God's word will again raise up prophets who cry "Prepare the way," with a deep hope that God will lead us by the "light of his glory, / with his mercy and justice for company" (Bar 5:9).

Praying with Scripture

- During Advent, express to God in prayer your deepest desires and hopes, for they have been placed by God in your heart.

- Pray about those "signs of the times" that most challenge the Church today.

- Pray in memory and hope about those prophetic figures who have prepared the way for God to enter your life.

The Immaculate Conception
of the Blessed Virgin Mary

Readings: Gen 3:9-15, 20; Ps 98; Eph 1:3-6, 11-12; Luke 1:26-38

"The LORD has made his salvation known" (Ps 98:2).

GRACED AND GRACIOUS

This celebration is especially appropriate at the beginning of Advent, when we recall the two great figures of expectation who prepared for the coming of Christ: John the Baptist and Mary. Forming a virtual liturgical "Ode to Joy," the readings resound with affirmations of the gracious love of God showered on Mary and on all who believe in her Son. The formal feast dates from the declaration made by Pope Pius IX on December 8, 1854, that Mary from the first moment of her conception was, by the singular grace and privilege of God and the merits of Jesus Christ, preserved from all stain of sin. Yet Mary's sinlessness had ancient roots in the Church, and in 1846 the U.S. bishops had chosen her as patroness of this land under the title of the Immaculate Conception.

While this feast is often confused in popular piety with the virgin birth of Jesus, which the gospel announces, the feast does not suggest that Mary was herself conceived in any miraculous manner. The greeting of Gabriel that Mary is a recipient of God's favor and gracious love, "full of grace," captures the meaning of the feast. Mary is one who does not turn away from God (Thomas Aquinas's definition of sin) and is totally open to God's love, captured in her final words: "I am the handmaid of the Lord. May it be done to me according to your word."

While celebrating the unique sinlessness of Mary, the feast should not detract from Mary's humanity. All the Gospels picture Mary as somewhat puzzled by her son's mission; her son will be a sign of contradiction, and a sword will pierce her heart; she will suffer the horrible pain of a mother watching a brutal execution.

The reading from Ephesians reminds us that a graced and blessed life is also God's plan for every Christian. God chose us to be "blessed in Christ" before the foundation of the world and destined us for "adoption to himself through Jesus Christ." The fullness of God's grace and love that embraces Mary from the first moment of her existence is to touch every Christian. We celebrate this feast with Mary as model and companion along our pilgrim journey toward the total embrace of God's love and grace.

PRAYING WITH SCRIPTURE

- Pray quietly the Hail Mary, pausing over those words that bring Mary into your life.

- In moments of doubt, hear again the words to Mary, "Do not be afraid, Mary, for you have found favor with God."

- As God leads you in new directions, exclaim with Mary, "May it be done to me according to your word."

Third Sunday of Advent

Readings: Zeph 3:14-18a; Isa 12:2-3, 4, 5-6 (Resp); Phil 4:4-7;
Luke 3:10-18

> **"Rejoice! Your kindness should be known to all"**
> **(Phil 4:4-5).**

WAITING FOR THE GOOD NEWS

For seven years I taught in Nashville, Tennessee, which is known not only for its rich musical tradition but also as a place where biblical religion is vital in people's lives. Riding along one day, I saw on a church bulletin board the Sunday sermon announced: "Repent, for the End is Near!" The topic for the Wednesday evening service was "The Bible and Financial Security!" My initial and somewhat unkind reaction was mentally to write in after the word "Near": "If Not, Come Wednesday." Yet as I reflect on Luke's Gospel for the Third Sunday of Advent, I see the need for repentance in the face of the ultimate fragility of this world, joined to an exhortation that our salvation is intertwined with a just use of material possessions.

In today's gospel (unfortunately truncated by the omission of Luke 3:7-9), John, the fiery, uncompromising reformer, first lashes out at those who come to be baptized: "Brood of vipers! Who warned you to flee from the coming wrath?" (Luke 3:7). He then tells them that their election as children of Abraham will do little good without the fruits of repentance; for every tree that does not bear fruit will be thrown into the fire. John later resumes this theme when he points to the coming "mightier one" (Jesus), whose "winnowing fan is in his hand to clear his threshing floor," so the chaff will be burned with unquenchable fire (Luke 3:17).

Yet in the middle of this passage John is strangely moderate. He urges people to use their possessions kindly and justly, telling the crowds to share their clothing with those in need, advising hated tax collectors simply to be honest in collecting taxes, and soldiers not to exploit people and to be content with their (often minimal) wages. Since these verses are found only in Luke, most likely the evangelist inserted them here to adjust John's teaching to one of the major themes of the Gospel and Acts; namely that great wealth can be an obstacle to following Jesus, while proper use of goods should characterize the true disciple.

Hearing John's preaching, we might ask, Where is the joy that runs through the first and second readings? Coming wrath and unquenchable fire are dubious reasons to rejoice. Still, as a figure of expectation for Jesus, John must have been disappointed. Jesus did not come onto the scene thundering threats of judgment but preaching good news to the poor, liberty to captives, sight for the blind, and freedom for those oppressed. Jesus' first contact with tax collectors is not to exhort them to honesty, but to call them to be disciples and then to have meals with them—so much so that he will be called "a glutton and a drunkard, a friend of tax collectors and sinners" (Luke 7:34).

Jesus' way of bringing people to God is different from John's. Jesus identifies himself as the Son of Man who has come "to seek and to save the lost"; he eats with sinners and tells parables of a God who searches for them when lost (Luke 15). Where John urges acts of conversion and repentance as a condition for communion with God, Jesus practices communion as a prelude to a deep experience of God's love.

There is much to rejoice about this Sunday, as we prepare to celebrate again the birth of God's Son, who will "renew you in his love" (Zeph 3:17). The readings tell us that no one is to be left out of this renewal. The Church, like Jesus, is summoned to practice communion with, and acceptance of, those whom our society would reject.

Recently a bishop who had begun a hostel for AIDS victims was asked why money was spent to care for such people, many of whom were not Catholics. He responded that we do not help suffering and oppressed people because *they are* Catholic but because *we are*. A good Advent thought.

Praying with Scripture

- Place yourself before John with the crowds. What might he say to you at this time?

- Zephaniah says, "Be not discouraged," and Paul, "Have no anxiety." Place your fears and anxiety before God.

- Pray about how you might imitate Jesus by accepting others as a sign of God's love and mercy.

Fourth Sunday of Advent

Readings: Mic 5:1-4a; Ps 80; Heb 10:5-10; Luke 1:39-45

"Blessed are you who believed" (Luke 1:45).

I Sing of a Maiden

Luke's infancy narratives have shaped the Catholic imagination and inspired Christian art through the centuries, providing a series of verbal icons as we contemplate again the mystery of the Word made flesh. The visit of Mary to Elizabeth in today's gospel is often depicted in art, with these two women in a wordless embrace, sharing, like all mothers-to-be, the mystery of new life within themselves, with a sense of mutual awe over what God has done.

The gospel is a treasure-trove of Lukan themes. Carrying Jesus within herself, Mary sets out on a journey from Nazareth to the hill country of Judea, anticipating that final journey that Jesus will make from Nazareth to his death in Jerusalem. Immediately Elizabeth greets Mary; the child leaps for joy in her womb, reflecting a biblical motif that the action of a child in the womb anticipates future destiny (Gen 25:22-23). John will be the first to recognize the presence of Jesus as he begins his public ministry. Elizabeth, then, like the prophets of old and like Mary, is filled with the Holy Spirit and proclaims God's word, "Blessed are you among women," echoing Gabriel's greeting to Mary. Then she pronounces a second blessing on Mary, "Blessed are you who believed that what was spoken to you by the Lord would be fulfilled." This blessing anticipates Luke 11:27-28, where a woman cries out, "Blessed is the womb that carried you and the breasts at which you nursed," only to have Jesus respond, "Rather, blessed are those who hear the word of God and observe it." Elizabeth's praise describes Mary as the model believer in Luke's Gospel. She believes in the word of God that has been spoken to her and acts on that word in her journey to Elizabeth. Mary is truly the "Mother of the Church," a pilgrim Church called to believe God's word and to follow it in its own journeys.

PRAYING WITH SCRIPTURE

- The joyful mysteries of the Rosary follow the key events of the Lukan infancy narratives. Pray these mysteries during this season.

- Amid the rush and commercialism of the season, quietly ponder in your heart the extraordinary gifts of God given to you and your loved ones.

- Pray especially for expectant mothers during this season.

December 25

The Nativity of the Lord (Christmas)
Mass at Midnight

Readings: Isa 9:1-6; Ps 96; Titus 2:11-14; Luke 2:1-14

"Let the heavens be glad and the earth rejoice"
(Ps 96:11).

CHRISTMAS POETRY

The readings for Christmas Midnight Mass are a liturgy in poetry that has shaped Christmas devotion through the ages. A mood of joyful surprise runs throughout: "Upon those who dwelt in the land of gloom / a light has shone" (Isa 9:1); "The grace of God has appeared, saving all" (Titus 2:11); "I proclaim to you good news of great joy" (Luke 2:10). This is not the superficial, feel-good joy marketed by the media from Thanksgiving through Christmas. Isaiah writes during a period of war against Judea by a coalition of enemies and the expansion of the Assyrian empire, which will spell the downfall of the Northern Kingdom. Yet Isaiah promises the birth of a child-king who will secure the Davidic line, in a way different from war and political alliances. The accoutrements of war will be burned as fuel for the flames, and this child will be "Wonder-Counselor, God-Hero, / Father-Forever, Prince of Peace" (Isa 9:5).

"In those days" marks the solemn beginning of the gospel; the census underscores that Jesus is born in a land under foreign occupation. Joseph and Mary, in the late stages of her pregnancy, make an arduous journey from Nazareth to the city of David, and Mary gives birth most likely in a cave or temporary shelter, since they cannot not find a place even in the somewhat primitive travelers' hostel. The child's first crib is an animal's feeding trough. A migrant couple, alone and without relatives and friends, gaze on their newborn child.

The gospel culminates in the message to the shepherds: "Do not be afraid; for behold, I proclaim to you good news of great joy that will be for all the people." A savior is born in David's city, and like the other son of David, Solomon, he is wrapped in swaddling clothes (Wis 7:4). The names given to Jesus—savior, anointed one (Christ), Lord—that celebrate his birth were customarily applied to imperial figures, like Augustus. Jesus' birth is not proclaimed to regal courtiers but to people of little regard, rural shepherds. In place of a proclamation sent through the empire that a royal birth brings peace, the messengers of God proclaim God's glory and peace on earth to all people who have now received God's favor.

Like the heavenly multitude, a multitude of reflections arise. Jesus' birth is good news for all people; humanity is radically changed; words of hope are proclaimed to a subject people; a peace is offered that casts out fear. Outsiders—shepherds—are the first heralds of Jesus' birth, as will be Anna in Luke 2:38. Mary, who does not speak, hears the proclamation and treasures their words in her heart. Like every mother, she gazes upon her newborn and wonders what this child will be. She is a model of one who, even in the presence of God's extraordinary events, ponders their deeper meaning, a task that remains God's gift to us on Christmas day.

PRAYING WITH SCRIPTURE

- Repeat in prayer the words of the angel: "Do not be afraid, for behold, I proclaim to you good news of great joy."

- Pray that God's gift of peace may descend upon our violent world.

- Pray especially for children on this day when we recall the Word made flesh as a helpless infant.

The Holy Family of Jesus, Mary, and Joseph

Readings: Sir 3:2-6, 12-14 or 1 Sam 1:20-22, 24-28; Ps 84; Col 3:12-21 or 3:12-17 or 1 John 3:1-2, 21-24; Luke 2:41-52

"Son, why have you done this to us?" (Luke 2:48).

WORDS TO LIVE BY; A LIGHT TO GUIDE

The Christmas-Epiphany cycle offers a series of windows into the mystery of the birth and manifestation of Jesus rather than a sequential tour through the infancy narratives. The already rich fare of the Christmas season was expanded within the last century by the addition of the feast of the Holy Family, now celebrated on the first Sunday after Christmas. Multiple themes characterize the readings: a woman dedicating her child to God; a young Jesus in the temple astounding learned teachers, while perplexing his parents as he follows his Father's will. The reading from 1 John points to a quality of love that can sustain family life.

The first reading could better be called "Hannah's Story," since it is told from her perspective and unfolds from her initiative (I recommend reading the whole of 1 Samuel 1:1–2:11). As in the story of Mary over a millennium later, the conception and birth of a son occur through God's intervention; but after the birth, when Hannah's husband Elkanah was going up to offer sacrifice, Hannah tells him that she will wait to go up later so that she can dedicate the child to God. In a response that could well guide family life today, he says, "Do what you think best" (1 Sam 1:23). She then goes up to Shiloh with a sacrifice, which Elkanah enacts, but then approaches Eli the priest and says, "I am the woman who stood near you here, praying to the LORD. . . . Now I, in turn, give him to the LORD" (1 Sam 2:1). She then prays a canticle that begins like Mary's: "My heart exults in the LORD." Hannah is a parade example of an assembly of women in the Hebrew Bible whose faith and courage make possible the unfolding of salvation history.

Today's gospel has been variously titled "The Finding of the Boy Jesus in the Temple," "The Boy Jesus in Jerusalem," and "Jesus Among the Teachers." The story accents three aspects of Luke's theology. The family of Jesus are faithful and observant Jews, who annually make the Passover pilgrimage to Jerusalem. Jesus is himself a teacher; expounding the Scriptures will characterize his public life. His commitment to God here transcends human expectation and Jewish piety. The center of the narrative is really the loss and finding of Jesus and the dialogue with Mary, who, like Hannah, speaks instead of the father; yet she expresses the "anxiety" of both of them. Jesus responds with a double-meaning phrase that can be translated "I must be in my Father's house" or "I must be about my Father's business." The gospel concludes with a twofold reaction: Jesus returns with Mary and Joseph and grows in wisdom, age, and favor [with God], while Mary, as she did earlier (see Luke 2:19), keeps these things in her heart.

The readings offer a realistic challenge to family life today, and not simply by emphasizing the virtues of fidelity to God, obedience, and growth in wisdom. Every parent is faced in a different manner with the surprise that Mary feels. As children mature after long years of love and guidance, the emerging adults begin to forge their own paths. Like Mary and Joseph, parents often cannot understand what they say, and yet Jesus' journey to self-understanding begun at Jerusalem concludes with a return to the support and love of Nazareth. Today's readings can comfort parents with the wisdom that their journeys are not unique or without companions.

PRAYING WITH SCRIPTURE

- Recall various journeys in your life, praying about the gift and mystery of family.

- Parents with recently born children might pray with Hannah and Mary as they dedicate their children to God.

- The Letter of John describes those who have believed in Christ as "children of God." Pray that this deep interior union may continue to be expressed by Christians today.

January 1

Solemnity of the Blessed Virgin Mary, the Mother of God

Readings: Num 6:22-27; Ps 67; Gal 4:4-7; Luke 2:16-21

"And Mary kept all these things, reflecting on them in her heart" (Luke 2:19).

"GOD'S INFINITY; DWINDLED TO INFANCY" (Gerard Manley Hopkins)

This feast provides the necessary symmetry to the mystery of the Incarnation: "the Word became flesh / and made his dwelling among us" (John 1:14). Mary was the flesh and blood from which the human body of Jesus was formed; his first dwelling was in her womb. So profound is this mystery that at the conclusion of the Council of Ephesus (A.D. 431), crowds streamed through the streets shouting, *"Theotokos, Theotokos,"* ("God-bearer," or Mother of God). A Son of God, "born of a woman" (Gal 4:4), heralds St. Paul, and no male in history, be he saint, sinner, pauper, or pope, can claim such a privilege.

Devotion to Mary is as much part of Catholicism as the Incarnation itself, but it has taken myriad forms throughout the centuries, captured in the cadences of the ancient Litany of the Blessed Virgin: "Holy Mother of God . . . Virgin of Virgins . . . Mother of Divine Grace . . . Mother Most Amiable . . . Mother Most Merciful . . . Mirror of Justice . . . Seat of Wisdom . . . Mystical Rose . . . Tower of Ivory . . . Morning Star . . . Health of the Sick . . . Refuge of Sinners . . . Comforter of the Afflicted." This mystery strains the human imagination while enriching it. Mary, the woman from whom divine life on earth was formed, embodies those experiences of God that accompany the human pilgrimage. She is a young woman fearful but courageous in the face of a divine call (Luke 1:29), a mother distraught at the disappearance of a teen-aged son (Luke 2:46), and wrestling with his adult chosen way of life (Mark 3:31). She walks in deep faith with him (John 2:4-5) and is broken at the cross with him as his life blood pours out

(John 19:25, 34), the blood that first coursed through her veins. Mary watches quietly with mothers around the world today who sit beside dying children, limbs shattered and bodies bleeding from yet another onslaught of violent death.

One of the paradoxes of contemporary theology is that while there has been a "reappropriation" of Mary as the ideal disciple of Jesus, one who hears God's word and acts upon it while treasuring God's mysteries in her heart, the "motherhood" of Mary is often played down even among feminist theologians. Much of this may be due to a romantic evaluation of motherhood by a male hierarchy as well as to a use of this sublime vocation to preclude women from full participation in Church life. Sister Mary Aquin O'Neill, R.S.M., director of Mount Saint Agnes Theological Center for Women, comments that a true vision of Mary's motherhood provides the basis of an anthropology that counters the old taboos about women's bodies as impure, a source of temptation and threat. Her motherhood demonstrates that "female embodiment is compatible with divinity and can be a symbol of God." She also remarks that before Mary was Jesus' disciple, "he learned from her." Mary nurtured him, taught him about the religious traditions of his people, and guided him through childhood (see "Female Embodiment and the Incarnation," in Francis Eigo, *Themes in Feminist Theology for the New Millennium* [Villanova, Pa.: Villanova Univ. Press, 2002]).

While honoring Mary on this day as Mother of God, we might recall that during the Second Vatican Council, Pope Paul VI called her "Mother of the Church." Mary is also a model of the Church as mother. Long ago St. Ambrose exhorted his congregation: "Let Mary's soul be in each of you to proclaim the greatness of the Lord. Let her spirit be in each to rejoice in the Lord. Christ has only one mother in the flesh, but we all bring forth Christ in faith" (*Liturgy of the Hours*, Office of Readings, December 21). On this octave of Christmas all Christians may pray in gratitude for God-bearing women and can reflect that they, too, have conceived Christ in their hearts and are called to bring him forth to a suffering world.

PRAYING WITH SCRIPTURE

- Ask Mary for a deeper understanding of her vocation to be the Mother of God.

- Pray that the Church may treasure in its heart the gifts of women.

- In prayer, think of those countless mothers who stand by the cross of suffering and death.

The Epiphany of the Lord

Readings: Isa 60:1-6; Ps 72; Eph 3:2-3a, 5-6; Matt 2:1-12

"Upon you the Lord shines,
and over you appears his glory" (Isa 60:2).

Following a Young Star!

A number of years ago on Epiphany eve, I was visiting a stellar family with four exuberant little boys ranging in age from eight to two. Johnny, age five, and I were looking through the family Christmas cards, and he seemed especially fascinated by the varied and elaborate illustrations of the magi, camels, sparkling gifts, and sundry potentates. Yet he became a bit pensive and a little sad, so I asked, "What's wrong, Johnny?" He blurted out, "No girls!"

I was reminded then of Isaiah's statement, "A little child shall lead them," for Johnny had really captured the meaning of the Epiphany, or "showing forth," of Jesus. In Matthew's Gospel the message is clear: Christ is for all people. Wise men or "astrologers" from the East, led by their own probing of heavenly mysteries, come to the newborn Jesus. They are Gentiles to whom the risen Jesus will send his disciples. The good news that begins with the birth of Jesus and continues after his death and resurrection is to include all people.

Throughout Christian history the journey of the magi has been variously portrayed in sculpture, visual art, medieval pageants, and contemporary dramas. Matthew's night visitors—who are neither three nor kings—gradually become kings, increase in number, are depicted as young, middle-aged, and old, and include people of color. The bounds of universality and inclusiveness are extended. Johnny was right in asking, "Where are the girls?" since the gift of God in Jesus is to transcend national, social, and gender differences (see Gal 3:28-29).

The religious map of the United States is dramatically changing, and the traditional Jewish and Christian populations are supplemented by a strong increase in the number of Muslims and followers of Eastern

18

religions. The Epiphany tells us that God is a light for all peoples and that peoples acting on their own wisdom and in their own time are making journeys led by God's light. These may end up in a manner as surprising to us as it was to the original visitors, who were "overjoyed at seeing the star."

PRAYING WITH SCRIPTURE

- Pray over ways in which God's light has guided you to new encounters with God.

- Prayerfully consider ways in which the Church might better witness to God's all-inclusive love.

- Pray for our brothers and sisters of the Eastern Orthodox Churches, who celebrate Christmas today.

Sunday after January 6

The Baptism of the Lord

(First Sunday in Ordinary Time)

Readings: Isa 42:1-4, 6-7; Ps 29; Acts 10:34-38;
Luke 3:15-16, 21-22

"A covenant of the people,
a light for the nations"
(Isa 42:6).

SENT FORTH BY THE SPIRIT OF GOD

With this feast the proclamation of the "Word made flesh," which brings joy to all people, moves to the unfolding narrative of the historical life of Jesus. In each Gospel the baptism of Jesus is both his public manifestation and his commission to fulfill the Father's will, and each tints the scene with a distinctive theological coloring. Luke enhances the theme of eager anticipation that permeates the infancy narratives, when "all the people" are asking in their hearts whether John might be the Christ. As one whose mission is to prepare for and point to the Messiah, John heralds the coming of the "one mightier" who will baptize with the Holy Spirit and fire—a prediction fulfilled only at Pentecost. The whole liturgical cycle is here in embryonic form.

Strangely, however, Luke does not recount explicitly that Jesus was baptized by John, who in Luke 3:20 (a verse omitted from the Lectionary) is imprisoned by Herod *before* the baptism of Jesus. Rather, he stresses that Jesus was baptized only after all the people and "was praying" when the heaven opened and the Holy Spirit descended upon him and he received the commission as Son and Servant. Jesus at prayer is particular to Luke and foreshadows the importance of prayer throughout the Gospel and Acts. In Luke-Acts, major events of salvation history occur in the context of prayer (for example, the annunciation to Zechariah, the Transfiguration, the death of Jesus), and the major figures of the Gospel are people who proclaim God in prayer

(Mary and Zechariah) and model lives of quiet prayer (Anna and Simeon). The pattern continues in the Acts of the Apostles (for example, 2:42-47; 3:1; 7:59-60; 9:11). Only Luke has the parables of prayer (11:5-8; 18:1-14). Jesus' life and history unfold from Spirit-inspired prayer, as will the lives of his followers.

Today's readings stress also the universal importance of Jesus' commission as the servant Messiah. Luke sees Jesus as the fulfillment of Isaiah's "servant whom I [the Lord] uphold, my chosen one with whom I am well pleased." This servant "shall bring forth justice *to the nations*" [emphasis added], but he will not do this by "crying or shouting out" or even by breaking a bruised reed; rather, he will establish justice by his teaching. As servant, Jesus will be both covenant and light, and the reader of Luke cannot but perceive that Jesus will become such a covenant when his lifeblood is poured out on the cross.

The reading from Acts offers a remarkable perspective on the baptism of Jesus. It concludes a sequence of events that begins with Peter somewhat hungry "at prayer" on the roof of the house of Simon the Tanner. He has a remarkable vision of animals and reptiles forbidden for human consumption descending from the sky only to hear a voice say, "Get up, Peter. Slaughter and eat." After Peter protests that he has never eaten anything "unclean," the voice proclaims, "What God has made clean, you are not to call profane" (Acts 10:13-15). Emissaries of the Gentile centurion Cornelius, who invite Peter to visit, then interrupt the story. Upon arriving, Peter finds that Cornelius, too, had a vision while at prayer, telling him to summon Peter.

Cornelius's account evokes Peter's speech, which is recounted in the second reading today. It is a clarion call to universalism. Peter's vision has shown him that the food laws, which were so central to Jewish identity, should not preclude the acceptance of Gentiles. God "shows no partiality," and in every nation "whoever fears him and acts uprightly is acceptable to him" (Acts 10:34-35). Only then does Peter summarize the career of Jesus, beginning with his baptism and continuing as he went about doing good and healing the oppressed. The account, called often "the Pentecost of the Gentiles," will then conclude with the baptism of Cornelius and the descent of the Spirit on all those assembled there.

Like the food descending from heaven in Acts 10, today's readings offer a rich banquet. Jesus' baptism is also his mission to be the chosen servant who will embody and proclaim a way of justice, peace, and liberation. Of all the Gospels, Luke's emphasizes that this quest for justice must unfold in a non-violent manner that involves acceptance of the marginal and excluded (for example, the Samaritans) and culminates in forgiveness of enemies. Christians today should think of their own baptism as a mission and commission to be a light to the nations.

In Acts the community now baptized "with the Holy Spirit and power" is a community that will continue to break through ethnic and religious barriers. Today we may think of the food laws as archaic and not significant, but for a first-century Jew like Peter they carried the moral authority of revelation and centuries of tradition, highlighted by his protest about never eating unclean food. As the Church today is summoned in unprecedented fashion to be a light for the nations and to seek "in every nation" those who do good, it must be willing to question which traditions are a hindrance, no matter how seemingly sacred, in light of where God's Spirit may be leading. The last twenty years have seen a massive recentralization of liturgical life and theological adaptation by the Roman Curia. It may be time for a hungry community to pray on the roof.

Praying with Scripture

- Look at a lighted candle and recall your baptism and mission to be a light to the world.

- Prayerfully recall that through baptism we become those with whom God is well pleased.

- As God proclaimed peace through Jesus Christ, pray that Christians will be instruments of peace.

Second Sunday in Ordinary Time

Readings: Isa 62:1-5; Ps 96; 1 Cor 12:4-11; John 2:1-11

"Announce his salvation, day after day" (Ps 96:2).

A WEDDING SURPRISE!

In the early Church the Epiphany cycle included other manifestations of Jesus—his baptism and the wedding at Cana. Today's liturgy focuses on the third manifestation, the wedding feast at Cana, the first of Jesus' signs, that is, symbols of the divine power at work in the Incarnate Word. The gospels this Sunday and next provide distinct pictures of Jesus' inauguration of his public ministry.

The narrative does not stress the miraculous changing of water into wine, which is not described but implied in the question of the headwaiter. This transformation is a sign of the deeper transformation that will occur in John's Gospel. The narrative culminates with the words: "[at] the beginning of his signs . . . " Jesus revealed his glory, and "his disciples began to believe in him." The reaction of the disciples and the interaction between Jesus and his mother provide dramatic focus to the narrative. Jesus begins his public ministry as a young couple begin their life together. When the wine begins to run out, Jesus' mother notes this and receives a seeming rebuke, "Woman, how does your concern affect me? My hour has not yet come." Often commentators soften the response of Jesus, but it is couched in terms of rebuke, using the exact same phrase that Jesus uses in Mark to rebuke a demon (Mark 1:24; 5:7; literally, "What is there in common between me and you?") In John's Gospel Jesus is "from above," and no human, not even those closest to him, understands him completely. Yet, Mary remains a stirring model of faith in face of this mystery. She immediately says, "Do whatever he tells you," and the sign is accomplished. Mary is a symbol of many people who have great faith in Jesus but do not really understand who he is.

Yet, Mary's faith will lead to the true manifestation of the glory of Jesus, since the reference to the hour points to the lifting up on the cross, when he will draw all people to himself (John 8:28; 12:32), and to that moment when Mary will embody discipleship in its fullness. Mary's birth pangs in John occur at the cross as she becomes "the mother" of all those whose love leads them to Jesus, epitomized by the presence of "the disciple whom Jesus loved."

The reading from Isaiah uses the metaphor of spousal love to describe God's love for the people. The wedding feast at Cana not only narrates the first sign of Jesus but is rich in biblical symbolism. The coming of the Messiah is often portrayed as a wedding banquet (see Matt 22:1-14; 25:1-3). The amount of fine wine given by Jesus equals between 120 and 180 gallons, which reflects the Old Testament motif of an abundance of wine in the final days (Amos 9:13-14; Hos 14:8; Jer 31:12). This first sign is the manifestation of the grace and truth that have come through Jesus Christ (John 1:17) and a summons to join in the celebration.

PRAYING WITH SCRIPTURE

- At those times when Jesus seems to turn away from your prayers, think of the faith of Mary.

- Pray in a special way for those young couples beginning life together.

- Where today do we find signs of the work of Christ?

Third Sunday in Ordinary Time

Readings: Neh 8:2-4a, 5-6, 8-10; Ps 19; 1 Cor 12:12-30;
Luke 1:1-4; 4:14-21

"Your words, Lord, are Spirit and life" (Ps resp.).

A MANDATE FOR MISSION

The Lectionary continues the theme of the initial manifestations of
Jesus. The gospel joins the first words of Luke's Gospel to Jesus' initial
proclamation at Nazareth. Luke states that his purpose is to produce a
narrative or story, while he relies on traditions handed down by eye-
witnesses and "ministers of the word." Throughout this liturgical cycle
we will be enriched by the insights from Luke's Gospel.

In the second part of today's gospel, Luke describes the beginning of
Jesus' ministry differently than the other evangelists, who begin with
Jesus calling his first disciples. In Luke, Jesus arrives in Galilee "in the
power of the Spirit," teaches, and delivers his inaugural sermon in
Nazareth. He roots his mission and ministry in the written word of Isaiah, where the Spirit sends the prophet to bring glad tidings to the poor,
liberation to captives, recovery of sight to the blind, and freedom for
the oppressed—language that reflects the biblical jubilee year (the traditional release of debts and return of property to its owners every fifti-
eth year). Jesus' sense of mission is an overture to his teaching and
actions throughout the Gospel and to the mission of the early Church
in Acts. When the contemporary Church concludes a year of jubilee,
the Gospel reminds us that the Church must continually renew the true
jubilee of concern for the marginal and freedom for the oppressed. January is a season when various political leaders give their "inaugural addresses"; one might ask where are the kinds of people Jesus was
concerned about in his inaugural address at Nazareth?

A second major theme that characterizes our beginning journey
emerges from Paul's vision of a community which is composed of
people with many and diverse gifts, but which lives in interdependent

unity. Writing to a community at Corinth, where certain people prided themselves on their talents and gifts, Paul counters by saying that all parts of the body, even "the less presentable parts," are essential, for "God has so constructed the body as to give greater honor to a part that is without it, so that there may be no division in the body, but that the parts may have the same concern for one another." He then goes on to list a host of gifts and ministries (including "administration") without which the body of Christ cannot function. If the Church today is to preach the good news to the poor and liberation to captives, it too must be a union of people with different gifts, all of which are essential but not taken over by one group. Mutuality and interdependence, not subordination and privilege, must characterize Christ's body.

Combined with Nehemiah's proclamation of the law to the returning exiles, the importance and power of God's word is a third major motif of the readings. Recently Cardinal Carlo Martini of Milan called for "a renewal of the biblical renewal." Though Vatican II mandated that the proclamation, preaching, and study of Scripture were to be at the heart of Church life, the vitality of the biblical renewal seems to have been overwhelmed by a massive increase in official teaching and theological reflection. Also, at home and at work Catholics are faced with literalist readings of Scripture. Overworked priests and bishops find it difficult to dedicate the time and energy to prepare challenging biblical homilies. Paradoxically and thankfully, Scripture remains vital among those non-ordained "ministers of the word" through things such as the RCIA, parish study groups, and summer Scripture institutes.

If the spirit of the jubilee is to continue, the Church must renew its commitment to live and study the Word of God and explore other ways in which more Catholics living the Gospel may become truly "ministers of the word," and so manifest the diversity of gifts of the Spirit described by St. Paul to the Corinthians.

PRAYING WITH SCRIPTURE

- Pray over how the coming year may be a time of celebration of God's new creation.

- Pray quietly with 1 Corinthians 12, recalling the gifts of the Spirit that have been given to you and how they build up Christ's body.

- Prayerfully consider other ways in which devotion to God's word in Scripture may be renewed.

Fourth Sunday in Ordinary Time

Readings: Jer 1:4-5, 17-19; Ps 71; 1 Cor 12:31–13:13; Luke 4:21-30

"Love never fails" (1 Cor 13:8).

TOUGH LOVE

Today's readings exemplify the diversity of Scripture. Jeremiah and Luke express the strong biblical motif of the prophet called by God but opposed and rejected by those to whom he is sent. Each reading has overtones of violence. Jeremiah is told to gird up his loins, that he will be a "pillar of iron, a wall of brass." The gospel recounts not only the rejection of Jesus but an unsuccessful attempt to kill him. Yet the reading from Paul is the great hymn to love (a wedding favorite), in which Paul subordinates prophecy to love, which "endures all things."

The gospel tells "the rest of the story" from last week by recounting the enthusiastic reception of Jesus' inaugural sermon by his townsfolk (they "were amazed at the gracious words that came from his mouth"), only to have the mood suddenly change. The people seem surprised that the "hometown" boy can speak so eloquently. "Isn't this the son of Joseph?" The rejection escalates as Jesus reads their real thoughts: the people want him to do for them the kind of mighty works he performed in Capernaum. Jesus counters by quoting a well-known proverb, "No prophet is accepted in his own native place." In the Gospels Jesus is not accepted by his own family, and no disciple was a member of his family. The folks at Nazareth want a domesticated Jesus at their disposal.

Jesus then rubs salt into the wounds by telling two parallel stories of the prophets Elijah and Elisha. Elijah was one of the most heralded Israelite prophets. He was powerful in word and deed. Sirach says that he "arose like a fire, and his word burned like a torch" (Sir 48:1) [NSRV]. He was taken to heaven in a fiery chariot and was expected to return as precursor of the Messiah. Luke's Jesus calls attention to Elijah's gift of miraculous food to a widow from Zarephath (Sidon) during a famine and parallels this with a reference to the healing of a Syrian leper, Naaman, by Elijah's disciple Elisha. Hearing this, the townspeople try to kill Jesus.

Jesus here anticipates his mission in Luke. Later he will cleanse a leper (5:12-16) and raise the son of a widow (7:11-17). He himself will become the rejected prophet, a major theme of Luke's Gospel. Like John, who criticizes those who pride themselves on their descent from Abraham without bearing fruit, Jesus says that God's grace and power will benefit outsiders, anticipating the welcome given to Gentiles in Acts.

These readings challenge the Church today. Prophets are rarely accepted among their own. The pacifism of Dorothy Day, for example, was long an embarrassment to the hierarchy. Yet, when reflecting on the meaning of the Catholic Worker, she said, like Paul, that neither poverty nor community was its most important characteristic but "the final word is love. At times it has been, in the words of Father Zossima, a harsh and dreadful thing, and our very faith in love has been tried through fire," and that love of God comes from loving each other.

Archbishop Oscar Romero, a prophet for our age, was hated not simply because of his commitment to liberation theology and his advocacy on behalf of the poor but because he was seen as turning away from the upper classes, who felt that the Church was "their own."

These two prophets, Dorothy Day and Archbishop Romero, were living embodiments of Paul's hymn to love and have received (perhaps with a bit of heavenly embarrassment) that worldwide honor once denied them.

PRAYING WITH SCRIPTURE

- In those moments when misunderstanding by one's family and friends causes great pain, ask Jesus for the strength to move forward.

- Pray Paul's hymn to charity, substituting the name of Christ for the word "love."

- Pray that God will raise up prophets and leaders for our Church today.

Fifth Sunday in Ordinary Time

Readings: Isa 6:1-2a, 3-8; Ps 138; 1 Cor 15:1-11; Luke 5:1-11

"By the grace of God I am what I am" (1 Cor 15:10).

WHAT! ME A DISCIPLE?

Rarely are the three Lectionary readings so integrated as they are this Sunday. They all portray God's call, though in diverse and dramatic fashion. Isaiah, the confidant of kings, receives God's call in an overwhelming vision of the Holy One in the Temple and responds simply, "Here I am, send me!" Paul, the former persecutor and forgiven sinner, becomes an apostle, affirming that "by the grace of God, I am what I am." And the Gospel proclaims Luke's distinctive portrait of the call of the disciples.

The evangelists often communicate their theology by rearranging traditional material in ways that open up new vistas. In Luke's source (Mark), Jesus' first public act is to form a band of followers (Mark 1:16-20). Luke's Jesus gives his inaugural sermon, is rejected at Nazareth, then cures a demoniac and heals Simon's mother-in-law, though Simon himself has not yet appeared in the Gospel. Only then does Luke recount the call of the disciples. He does not describe them simply as a group that heeds Jesus' call to "Follow me" (as Mark and Matthew do). He rather tells the story of Jesus ordering a hesitant Simon to set out on a fishing expedition that results in a sensational catch, followed by Simon's plea for forgiveness and the words of Jesus to all the disciples: "Do not be afraid; from now on you will be catching [people]."

This sequence of material reflects Luke's theology. Jesus, the rejected prophet, turns like Elijah to outsiders and manifests his healing power. The disciples follow Jesus only after experiencing God's power, and then they turn their lives around, leaving everything to follow him. This provides the whole pattern for the early Church from Pentecost on, when the gift of the Spirit fills people with power, enables them to rejoice even amid persecution, and moves the Church outward to different peoples.

In both Luke and Paul, the call comes not to the virtuous and the dutiful but to sinners. Peter's reaction is not to follow Jesus but to shout, "Depart from me, Lord, for I am a sinful man." First in the parallel lists of those listed by Paul as first witnesses to the presence of the risen Lord are Kephas, who had previously denied Jesus, and James the brother of the Lord, who had not followed him in his lifetime, and the proclamation concludes with the call of Paul, "the least of the apostles," who had persecuted the Church of God. A profound experience of forgiveness goes hand in hand with the call to be a follower of Christ. In one of its recent General Congregations, the delegates posed the question, "What does it mean to be a Jesuit today?" Contrary to popular opinion that it might have been a *penchant* for fine Scotch or a love of travel, the document stated, "It is to know that one is a sinner, yet called to be a companion of Jesus, as Ignatius was." No sooner had the document been published than many Jesuits commented, "Well, this is simply what it means to be a Christian."

The three call stories tell of different ways in which the loving presence of God changed people's lives. Confronted by the massive challenges of life today and a culture often in opposition to the Gospel, the Church easily resorts to moralistic preaching. To be a Church in witness requires a prior experience of the surprising, forgiving, and overwhelming love of God. Only then can we all say, "Here I am, send me."

PRAYING WITH SCRIPTURE

- Pray with Paul's words, "By the grace of God, I am what I am," thinking of particularly graced times.

- In moments of guilt over sinfulness, recall that the Lord did not depart from Peter, but said, "Do not be afraid," and made him a disciple.

- Think of Isaiah and pray over those moments when the holiness of God seems overwhelming.

Sixth Sunday in Ordinary Time

Readings: Jer 17:5-8; Ps 1; 1 Cor 15:12, 16-20; Luke 6:17, 20-26

> **"Blessed the man who follows not the counsel
> of the wicked" (Lectionary).**

WEAL OR WOE

"Cursed" be the one who trusts in human beings; "the wicked" are like chaff that the wind drives away; "Woe" to you who are rich and filled now. Harsh words for a Sunday in gray February. They are unlike Matthew's nine blessings pronounced on the poor, the hungry, those who weep, and those who are persecuted. In Luke's Sermon on the Plain, four blessings are followed by four woes on the rich, the satiated, the scoffers, and the admired. Jesus here continues the theme of reversal in Mary's hymn, anticipating that God would put the mighty down from their thrones, exalt those of low degree, send the rich away empty, and fill the hungry with good things.

Luke's Gospel is often called the "Gospel for the Poor," since Jesus blesses those who are literally poor (6:20) rather than the poor in spirit (as does Matthew). Yet his blessing of the poor does not romanticize poverty, and the Gospel is more concerned to point out the dangers of wealth than to praise the virtues of the poor. The rich will be sent away empty; they have already received their consolation. Worldly cares, riches, and pleasures will choke the growth of God's word (8:16-20); the rich are motivated by greed and lack of concern for others, so they will be suddenly struck down at the very moment they gaze upon wealth stored up for many years and muse that it is time to eat, drink, and be merry (12:16-20).

In the parable of Dives and Lazarus (Luke 16:19-31), a wealthy man, dressed in royal purple and imported linen, is a parade example of conspicuous consumption. For him, every day was a banquet, while he did not even see the poor, starving, and sick Lazarus lying by his gate. When he finally saw him, the roles were reversed—the rich man was in

Hades and Lazarus was in heaven. Religious leaders are lovers of money (16:14); a would-be disciple cannot follow Jesus because he is "very rich" (18:23). The Acts of the Apostles attributes Judas's betrayal of Jesus to his desire for possessions (1:18); Ananias and Sapphira are struck down because their desire for money leads them to deceive the community (5:1-11); and Simon of Samaria is castigated by Peter because he tries to buy spiritual gifts (8:14-24).

It may be tempting to write off this harsh picture as a bit of first-century *ressentiment* or a touch of dour apocalyptic thinking by Luke's Jesus, but Luke's picture spoke to his community and still challenges the Church today. Luke does not offer a one-sided ethic. Though in the Gospel Jesus fulminates against the rich, in Acts the nascent Church shares goods instead of abandoning them; almsgiving is stressed (understood as an *obligation* to help the poor, not as an optional good deed); people of some means welcome Paul and share their resources (Acts 16:11-15; 17:12). In his final, moving speech to the Ephesians, Paul tells them to work to support the poor and weak (20:32-35).

Why this ambivalence? In his Gospel Luke tells a story of "roots." The Christian community, now led by the Holy Spirit, owes its origin to those who heard Jesus' word and followed in simplicity and poverty. They experienced the power and love of Jesus, which sustained them. By the time of the final composition of the Gospel and Acts, Luke's community seems to have included more and more people of some means. The voice of the Gospel warns them against the evil that springs from having and desiring great wealth. Luke offers the rich the good news that their salvation lies in concern for the poor and in using their goods for others.

Today's Church includes many people who leave everything to follow Christ, live in actual solidarity with poor people, and are insulted, hated, and persecuted for this. At the same time, the Church depends on the generosity of people of means to further its mission. The rich in the Gospel are by no means hard-working middle- or upper-middle-class people, but the arrogant and blind super-wealthy of imperial societies, reflected today in the super-rich or in global corporations. American Catholics, however, must never forget their roots and the danger that escalating upward mobility poses to faith. Great grandchildren of subway workers are CEOs of construction companies, often upset by those very unions for which their forebears fought; descendants of immigrants resent the large waves of "those people" moving into their neighborhoods. When the Church proclaims the option for the poor, this must be combined with critical reflection and prophetic witness about the dangers of the immense wealth that washes over sections of our country while the poor, mostly ignored in recent elections, struggle to remain afloat. In his powerful novel *The Sea Remains*, the priest-novelist Jean Sulivan lamented a Church that lived by "consoling the poor and reassuring the rich"—hardly a paraphrase of today's Gospel.

PRAYING WITH SCRIPTURE

- Pray about your "roots," thinking of those people today who share the same struggles as your forebears.
- Pray about your attitude toward riches and possessions, asking whether the Gospel or the culture shapes your values.
- Jeremiah calls blessed those who trust in the Lord; pray for a true spirit of trust.

Seventh Sunday in Ordinary Time

Readings: 1 Sam 26:2, 7-9, 12-13, 22-23; Ps 103; 1 Cor 15:45-49;
Luke 6:27-38

> **"Be merciful, just as your Father is**
> **merciful" (Luke 6:36).**

A WORLD WITHOUT ENEMIES?

As the religious landscape becomes more pluralistic, people, especially the young, wonder what is most characteristic of Christianity.

Today's gospel presents a paradox. Love of enemies, compassion,
mercy, and forgiveness appear as the core of Jesus' teaching in Luke's
Sermon on the Plain, with slight variations from Matthew's Sermon on
the Mount. Yet these qualities are often relegated to the margin of
Christianity. In 1927 Mahatma Gandhi, addressing a Christian group,
said: "If I had to face only the Sermon on the Mount and my own interpretation of it, I should not hesitate to say, 'Oh yes, I am a Christian.' . . . But negatively I can tell you that much of what passes as
Christianity is a negation of the Sermon on the Mount." It is a sad in-
dictment of Christianity that those who stress most its fundamentals
are often characterized by militarism, advocacy of capital punishment,
and bitterness toward opponents. No Christian group has adopted
Jesus' teaching on love of enemy as a critical test of orthodoxy.

Yet Jesus issues four ringing commands: Love your enemies; do
good to those who hate you; bless those who curse you; pray for those
who maltreat you. He then rejects a culture of violence characterized by
a tit-for-tat mentality and proposes instead a strategy of breaking the
cycle of evil. Again the command is repeated: Love your enemy and do
good. Why? The command is rooted in the very nature of God, who is
"kind to the ungrateful and the wicked" (Luke 6:35). Whereas Matthew
follows this exhortation with the statement: "Be perfect as your heavenly Father is perfect," Luke writes: "Be merciful, just as your Father is

merciful," and only then will you be sons and daughters of God. Love of enemies is the defining characteristic of God's family.

Love and mercy are often cheapened in common parlance. Love is not simply an emotion; it is a fundamental attitude that seeks another's good and responds to his or her need. Forsaking punishment does not constitute biblical mercy, which is, rather, compassionate love and concern, expressed beautifully in today's responsorial psalm: "He redeems your life from destruction, / crowns you with kindness and compassion." Luke's Good Samaritan, who rescues a half-dead traveler, shows mercy (10:37).

Luke's Jesus does not proclaim ethereal ideals but lives what he proclaims. The Lukan Jesus eats with and reaches out to those Pharisees who oppose him and, gives of himself to those who beg for healing or forgiveness. Only in Luke does Jesus, at the moment of his arrest, heal the wounded servant of the high priest, while calling for an end to any violent resistance (22:51); the dying Jesus prays, "Father, forgive them, they know not what they do" (23:34).

These commands can be dismissed as utopian or, worse, used by the powerful to exploit the weak. Even in the New Testament itself, slaves are told to love their masters, and abused spouses even today are often told to react with love and forgiveness rather than receive help. A true meaning of the love command is not acquiescence to evil and violence, but imitation of God's love by freeing enemies of their hatred and violent destructiveness, "to turn . . . the disobedient to the understanding of the righteous" (Luke 1:17). In his final words to his disciples, the risen Jesus sends them to proclaim conversion and the forgiveness of sin (Luke 24:46-47). Mercy and love, not evil, are to be regnant in human life. Love of enemies is not a substitute for the quest for a world of justice and peace, but its driving force. The nonviolent quest for justice and resistance to evil embodied by Gandhi or Martin Luther King, Jr., incarnates Jesus' love command.

Years ago Thomas Merton gazed upon the world's violence and wrote: "The beginning of the fight against hatred, the basic Christian answer to hatred, is not the commandment to love, but what must necessarily come before in order to make the commandment bearable and comprehensible. It is a prior commandment to believe. The root of Christian love is not the will to love, but the faith that one is loved," and "until this discovery is made, until this liberation has been brought about by the divine mercy, men and women are imprisoned in hate" (*New Seeds of Contemplation*). We who are often ungrateful and wicked, but who receive God's mercy and love, can now see in the face of the enemy the face of God.

PRAYING WITH SCRIPTURE

- Pray Psalm 103, savoring the mercy and compassion of God.
- Think of someone who has been "ungrateful and wicked," and pray that this person may experience God's goodness.
- Pray that the politics of forgiveness may supplant the politics of hatred.

Ash Wednesday

Readings: Joel 2:12-18; Ps 51; 2 Cor 5:20–6:2; Matt 6:1-6, 16-18

"A clean heart create for me, O God" (Ps 51:12).

LENT ALREADY

Ash Wednesday has become a virtual sacrament of Catholic identity as people throng to "get ashes," which, paradoxically, is just what the gospel counsels against—external signs of devotion. This day also begins not simply the forty days preceding Easter but the whole paschal cycle, which continues seven weeks after Easter until Pentecost. There is one mystery of the death of Jesus, his resurrection, and the gift of the Spirit. It is a time when the Church celebrates with joy the journey of new Christians to the baptismal font and the return of those whose life pilgrimages have led to strange detours and byways.

Today's gospel, like last Sunday's, stresses the need for interior renewal and integrity of prayer and action. The traditional practices of prayer, fasting, and almsgiving are not criticized; parading them as signs of religious devotion is what is reproved. Lent is a time for interior renewal, but this should be incarnate in practice. That is the message of the gospel and the wisdom of the Church.

In the brief reading from 2 Corinthians, St. Paul calls himself an ambassador of Christ, urging his community to be "reconciled to God." "Reconcile" in Greek means changing a state of hostility into one of unity and friendship. In the ancient world, reconciliation of political enemies involved the exchange of gifts, and in the next sentence Paul makes the extraordinary statement that "for our sake God made him to be sin who did not know sin," with the result that in Christ we become God's justice (NAB: "righteousness"). Reconciliation has a vertical dimension: humanity alienated from God by Adam's sin is now restored by Christ, the second Adam, who takes on the catastrophic results of this sin. It also has a horizontal dimension as Paul, throughout his letters, addresses disputes and differences in the fledgling Christian communities. The vertical and horizontal dimension meet in the cross of Christ. Lent prepares us to move toward that day when we celebrate the paradoxical victory of the Cross, life from death, an act of hatred transformed into a sign of love "for our sake" (2 Cor 5:21).

In the biblical and ecclesial tradition, repentance should be social as well as individual (in Jonah 3:8 not only all the Ninevites but even their cattle are covered with sackcloth and ashes). This Lent, as we receive ashes, we might pray over the horrible symbolism that ashes have carried in our century. The Holocaust will always imprint ashes in our memories and not simply on our foreheads. Ashes were all that remained of burned-out African-American churches. Ashes are a vivid reminder of the evils of racism and hatred of "the other," which seem endemic to our culture. During the jubilee year Pope John Paul II called for and enacted rituals of repentance for our complicity, intended or unintended, in the "culture of death." Lent also tells us that confession of sin and returning to a merciful God can change individuals and societies. Should we not give God a chance? That is what Lent is about.

PRAYING WITH SCRIPTURE

- Pray about ways that families and communities can better incorporate the Lenten journey into daily life.

- Ask God to create a new heart in our lives and societies, that we may turn away from the ashes of destruction to the light of Christ.

- Think of ways that we, like Paul, can be ambassadors of reconciliation.

First Sunday of Lent

Readings: Deut 26:4-10; Ps 91; Rom 10:8-13; Luke 4:1-13

> **"My refuge and fortress,
> my God in whom I trust" (Ps 91:2).**

GIVING THE DEVIL HIS DUE

The first two Sundays of Lent present the temptation and transfiguration of Jesus, which form a virtual epitome of the paschal mystery. Jesus, taking on human form, humbled himself even to death and was "tested" by his Father, yet this was a presage of his glorification. The next three Sundays in the Lukan cycle of readings stress themes of penance and conversion. The Old Testament readings recount those saving deeds of Israel's history that will again be heralded at the Easter Vigil. Compressed in the Lenten readings are themes, motifs, and figures that resound throughout Scripture. The Lenten pilgrimage is best made with Bible in hand.

While Mark narrates the "testing" of Jesus in two short verses, Matthew and Luke present elaborate narratives that weave together the dialogue between Jesus and the devil, a contest of scriptural interpretation and themes that foreshadow the subsequent career of Jesus and, in Luke, of the early Church. The testing of Jesus reflects the Old Testament theme of the testing of righteous people (for example Job), the servant of Isaiah 53, and the suffering just person, who, though tested by God, remains faithful and is called a child of God (Wis 2:12-20; 5:1-23). It also recalls the radical emptying of Jesus (Phil 2:5-11; Heb 2:18: "because he himself [Jesus] was tested through what he suffered, he is able to help those who are being tested)."

Luke stresses at both the beginning and end of the narrative that Jesus is "filled with the Holy Spirit," so the testing is enveloped by the presence of the Spirit. The testings emerge when the devil challenges Jesus to follow a path different from the one willed by his Father. Jesus is first tested to use his power to provide food for himself (much as

God provided food for the people in the wilderness); but in the first of three responses, all taken from Deuteronomy, Jesus says, "One does not live on bread alone" (cf. Deut 8:3). Jesus is then shown all the kingdoms of the world and their power and glory, which the devil will give him "if you worship me." Jesus responds with the most fundamental affirmation of Israel's faith, the first words of the Shema, "You shall worship the Lord, your God, and him alone shall you serve" (cf. Deut 6:13). Finally, on the pinnacle of the Temple in Jerusalem, Satan challenges Jesus (as in the first testing) to a miraculous demonstration of his power, and Jesus again invokes Deuteronomy (cf. 6:16), "You shall not put the LORD, your God, to the test."

This powerful narrative presents multiple challenges to appropriation today. Could Jesus really be put to the test by the devil? Is the world really under the devil's control? What was the fundamental test that Jesus faced? What do these have to do with Lent? Many Jewish writings close to the New Testament era, while affirming the absolute sovereignty of God, state that the "kingdoms of the world," with their proliferation of idolatry and brutal military rule, were Satan's domain. Luke anticipates the conflict of kingdoms that will unfold in his Gospel when Jesus will enact "release of captives" (4:18; 13:16) and cast out demons, and the early Church will practice "healing all those oppressed by the devil" (Acts 10:38). With Jesus' conquest of the devil, the ultimate victory of goodness over evil is assured, but the struggle will be renewed throughout history by Jesus' followers. In a world in which evil power is manifested today by humans in almost superhuman form (brutal, grasping dictators; structures of massive economic exploitation; the lust for violence), Luke's conflict of kingdoms seems quite contemporary.

Luke has a strong parallel between the first and third test. Both involve use of Jesus' power to save himself from suffering and death. That is the root meaning of these tests. Luke ends by noting that Satan leaves Jesus "for a time." The final test comes also in Jerusalem, on the cross, when again he is tempted three times to use his power to save himself. Jesus was tempted to follow a different kind of messiahship than the Father offered, one that would substitute demonstrations of power for rejection and suffering.

Such a "test" is the lot of followers of Jesus today. Our culture offers seemingly infinite possibilities for remaking one's self, with a priority put on personal fulfillment and material success. Christians are instead challenged to live not "by bread alone" (think of today's metaphor "bread" meaning money), to worship and serve God alone, and to discern and accept God's will in lives that seem often pedestrian and unimportant. But, as with Jesus, the trial of our lives begins with the embrace of the Spirit in baptism, unfolds in following Jesus' example in going through suffering and death to new life, again to be filled with the Spirit. This is the Lenten journey ever remembered, ever renewed.

PRAYING WITH SCRIPTURE

- Pray about ways in which the Church is especially "tested" today.

- The first reading is an exercise in anamnesis, or memorializing the acts of God. Create in prayer your own personal history of God's actions.

- Consider in prayer how Lent can be a time not of "doing" but of seeking God's will in your life.

Second Sunday of Lent

Readings: Gen 15:5-12, 17-18; Ps 27; Phil 3:17–4:1; Luke 9:28b-36

> **"Of you my heart speaks;**
> **you my glance seeks" (Ps 27:8).**

A VIEW FROM THE MOUNTAINTOP

The gospel this week is the second half of the diptych that presents Jesus' anticipated suffering (the temptation) and his ultimate exaltation (the transfiguration). All the Synoptic Gospels recount the transfiguration, but each has its distinctive accents. While Mark and Matthew locate it after Jesus begins his journey to Jerusalem, Luke locates it before Jesus "determined to journey to Jerusalem" (9:51). Only Luke places Jesus at prayer, and only in Luke is the conversation with Moses and Elijah about "his exodus that he was going to accomplish in Jerusalem." Luke also omits the term "transfigured" (*metamorphothé* in Greek), since Gentile readers could confuse it with pagan stories of metamorphoses in which various gods change shapes. Luke simply says that Jesus' face became different and his clothing dazzlingly white.

Distinct Lukan theological themes emerge. In the upcoming journey narrative (9:51–19:27), Luke includes the most distinctive material of his Gospel, such as the parables of the Good Samaritan, the Prodigal Son, the Widow and the Judge, the Pharisee and the Tax Collector, as well as significant teaching on discipleship and repentance. The Lukan transfiguration narrative functions, as does the appearance to Moses at the burning bush, as divine preparation and approval for his ministry of prophecy and teaching.

Like Moses, Jesus has deep encounters with God (see also Exod 34:29, where Moses' face shines "while he conversed with the LORD"). This also accords with Luke's stress on Jesus at prayer. Prayer is an opening to the mystery of God. All the major events of Jesus' life are preceded in Luke by a period of prayer (his baptism, the choice of the Twelve, the mission of the seventy-two disciples, his prayer in Gethsemane). Prayer characterizes major figures of the Gospel—Mary, Zechariah, Anna and Simeon; and in Acts all the "breakthroughs" in salvation history occur while people are at prayer (for example, Pentecost, Peter's vision at Caesarea). No surprise then that prayer, along with fasting and almsgiving, is one of the traditional practices of the Lenten journey.

The covenant with Abraham (first reading), while continuing the Lenten theme of remembrance of the great figures of salvation history, has an interesting connection with the gospel. Abraham places his faith and trust in God and is declared "righteous," but through God's covenant he is prepared for a journey that will take him from Ur of the Chaldees to the land of promise. He is to begin a journey and is transformed from "a wandering Aramean" into the parent of many nations.

Today Abraham is revered by the three great religions of the book— Christianity, Judaism, and Islam; yet in the Bible Abraham has faith, is declared righteous, and is given a mission by God before there is any Judaism, Christianity, or Islam. He is a symbol of the way God may touch people's lives and set them on a journey apart from established structures of belief.

After this transforming encounter, Jesus continues his journey, which unfolds as his teaching is met by carping opposition, frustration at dull-witted disciples, and concludes with his death, which is paradoxically his being taken up into the glory of the Father (Luke 9:51; 24:51).

Recently I read the compelling and beautifully written novel, *Lying Awake*, by Mark Salzman. (My pedestrian comments here are no substitute for engaging this remarkable book.) It tells of Sister St. John of the Cross, a Carmelite nun who is gifted with extraordinary experiences of God's presence, but also suffers from seizures and horrible headaches. Doctors diagnose temporal lobe epilepsy, which can be associated with mystical experiences, and Sister St. John is faced with the choice that the recommended surgery may free her from the pain and seizures but put an end to the "mountaintop" experiences of God. Transforming experiences of prayer have been her joy, but will she risk losing them as she continues her journey to God, perhaps in a more mundane way?

Lent reminds us every year that our lives are journeys, ultimately through death to new life, when "he will change our lowly body to conform with his glorifed body" (Phil 3:21). It also challenges us to deep experiences of prayer and a sense of God's presence that equip us for the daily, mundane, and often tedious journeys of our lives. The mountaintop remains in the background; vision is remembered rather than relived, and yet a voice rings in our ears: "This is my chosen Son; listen to him."

Is more needed?

PRAYING WITH SCRIPTURE

- Consider ways that prayer may become a constant part of your life journey.

- Thinking of Abraham, pray for greater understanding among Christians, Jews, and Muslims.

- Pray about journeys that await you and ask for God's transforming grace.

Third Sunday of Lent

Readings: Exod 3:1-8a, 13-15; Ps 103; 1 Cor 10:1-6, 10-12;
Luke 13:1-9

"Merciful and gracious is the Lord,
slow to anger and abounding in kindness" (Ps 103:8).

Spring Gardening

Shortly before Christmas in 1997, Harry Corcoran, a much beloved Jesuit, died. He was a charter member of the Catholic Theological Society of America and first dean of the Jesuit School of Theology at Berkeley, but above all, a shining person who walked constantly in God's presence. Once Harry was talking about his childhood and recalled his father saying, "Now Harry, I just want you to remember that God is a mighty unpredictable fellow." Harry's father anticipated, in less theological terms, Karl Rahner's constant refrain that God is absolute mystery.

Today's readings seem to present an unpredictable God. The first reading, one of the most significant in the Bible, narrates the self-revelation of God to Moses from the burning bush. Moses, the exiled shepherd, approaches a bush that burns without being consumed and hears a command to remove his shoes, since he is in a holy place (a custom still honored today when Muslims enter a mosque).

Then follows a series of startling divine self-disclosures. God is the God of the ancestors of the people, of Abraham, Isaac, and Jacob, and a God who enters into the history of a suffering people, expressed in a cavalcade of actions: I have witnessed their affliction and hear their cry and know well their suffering; I have come down to rescue them and to lead them out of a land of slavery to a land flowing with milk and honey. Israel's God is no otiose or disengaged monarch, but a loving parent who has compassion on his suffering children and enters their world as a liberator. As Abraham Joshua Heschel, the great Jewish theologian and mystic, often stressed, Israel's history is not so much

45

the story of suffering humanity's quest for God but of a compassionate God entering and shaping human life.

This God is then revealed to Moses by a name that is to be "remembered through all generations": "I am who am." The original impact of this powerful but enigmatic title has often been obscured by theological speculation. Name-giving is one of the most basic forms of communication, and here it carries the nuance of self-communication and abiding presence. It is not a description of God's essence so much as a promise of enduring presence, which summarizes the engaged God of the previous verses.

When we turn to the gospel, Jesus seems at first to show a different God. Murder by brutal rulers and accidental death seem to be divine punishment for sin, and Jesus says, "If you do not repent, you will all perish as they did!" Jesus' hearers shared a common worldview that sudden death was a punishment for sin, and that since things were going well in their lives, they had no need to repent. The point of comparison in the stories of the death of the Galileans and those killed by the falling tower is the suddenness of the event, not primarily that these events are divine punishment.

Jesus then adds a parable about a patient God who gives time for conversion. The owner of a fruitless fig tree wants it destroyed, but the vinedresser asks for more time to cultivate it so that "perhaps" it will bear fruit; but if not, it can be cut down. Jesus never tells what happened. Did the tree bear fruit? His hearers and we ourselves must answer that question in our own lives.

Today, and on the next two Sundays, the readings focus on the Lenten theme of repentance. Today's readings tell us that the God to whom we return (the root meaning of the word "repentance") is the God of our past, just as he was the God of Abraham and a God who constantly enters our lives with liberating compassion. Repentance, or a turning away from one path to another, is not so much finding God but being found by God. Jesus tells a parable of a God who is patient and ready to give a second chance. In God's time a fruitless past need not produce a barren future.

With the beginning of spring not far away, thoughts of gardening arise. Lent is a time for a little pruning and nurturing of our personal fig trees. After all, God is pretty unpredictable, and who knows what may blossom in a few weeks?

PRAYING WITH SCRIPTURE

- Repeat prayerfully and quietly the actions of God from the first reading.

- Pray about how God has entered your life in "unpredictable" ways.

- There is still time. In prayer inspect your personal "fig tree."

Fourth Sunday of Lent

Readings: Josh 5:9a, 10-12; Ps 34; 2 Cor 5:17-21;
Luke 15:1-3, 11-32

"Look to him that you may be radiant with joy"
(Ps 34:6).

THE PARDONER'S TALE

Today's readings are the second of the three Sundays before Holy Week, all of which stress the summons to return to God (repentance). Paul states the theme crisply: "The old things have passed away; behold, new things have come. And all this is from God, who has reconciled us to himself through Christ and given us the ministry of reconciliation." The gospel, called somewhat inaccurately "the parable of the Prodigal Son," has been described as "the gospel within the Gospel."

The story is a drama in three acts. Act One: A younger son asks for his share of the inheritance, goes off to a "distant country," squanders the money, suffers degradation and starvation, ends up feeding pigs and eating the garbage thrown to them. (He works for a Gentile and eats unclean food, thus denying his very heritage.) He then decides to return to his father, but is scarcely a model of repentance. His motivation is quite self-serving, "How many of my father's hired workers have more than enough food to eat, but here am I, dying from hunger." He resolves to return and prepares a little speech for his father: "Father, I have sinned against heaven and against you. I no longer deserve to be called your son; treat me as you would treat one of your hired workers." His journey home begins, and we can almost hear him reciting his program for forgiveness.

Act Two is the return of the prodigal. While he is still in the distance, his waiting father sees him, and "filled with compassion," he runs to his son, embraces and kisses him. Jesus' hearers would have gasped at the image of the father running, a strong cultural taboo in that society.

The son launches into his little speech, but in the embrace of the loving father one part of the speech is never uttered: "treat me as one of your hired workers." In another shocking gesture, the father orders the son clothed in a robe, ring, and sandals. Far from being welcomed as a servant, the son is restored to family dignity and given the signet ring to act with the father's authority.

When I first taught this parable, I wondered about the sandals, till I found that sandals were worn by free people while slaves went barefoot. Once an African-American student said to me, "Professor, you did not have to do all that research. Haven't you heard the spiritual that the slaves sang in hope of freedom, 'All God's children got shoes; all God's children have traveling shoes.'" Act Two ends, like all the parables in Luke 15, with a party. Finding must be celebrated.

In Act Three the spotlight is turned on the older brother. He is working the farm, as he has faithfully done for years. Hearing the unfamiliar sounds of partying, music, and dancing, he asks another servant to find out what is going on. When he hears that "your brother has returned," he becomes angry and sulks outside the house. In an action as shocking as his running and embracing the "little brother," the father goes out and pleads with his elder son, who, like his brother, has his own speech, but this time reeking with resentment. I have obeyed and served you "all these years," and "you never gave me even a young goat to feast on with my friends." The father does not debate the issue but simply says, "You are here with me always; everything I have is yours," but now come and celebrate and rejoice, because "your brother was dead and has come to life again; he was lost and has been found." The parable doesn't tell us whether he joined the party.

Despite their different life journeys, the younger and older sons have the same image of the father. The younger son thinks that the way to return to the father's good graces is to be treated as a servant; the older one boasts that all these years he has been a faithful servant. Both define sonship in terms of servile obligations; each in his own way destroys the family. The story is really a story of the "prodigal father," lavish in love, who shatters the self-understanding of both sons and wants both to be free. St. Paul puts it succinctly: "You are no longer slaves but sons and daughters, and if a son or daughter, then an heir through God" (Gal 4:7) [author's translation].

Living this parable becomes a challenge for our Lenten journey of return to a loving Father who breaks through our self-image of servants bent on pleasing a demanding master. This pardoning and prodigal God invites us to a family party freed from aimless wandering and resentful dutifulness.

PRAYING WITH SCRIPTURE

In prayer, identify with the characters of the parable:

- With the younger son, thinking that return is always possible and may contain some surprises.

- With the older brother, honestly facing those resentments which are often harbored even against God and which choke freedom and joy.

- With the father, thinking of the challenge to accept and change those who have offended or misunderstood you.

Fifth Sunday of Lent

Readings: Isa 43:16-21; Ps 126; Phil 3:8-14; John 8:1-11

"Neither do I condemn you"(John 8:11).

THE PUBLIC DEFENDER

As the sequence of Sundays proclaiming repentance draws to a close, the gospel presents one of the most graphic New Testament narratives on the mercy of Christ that leads to new life. The reading from Isaiah prepares the way as the Lord says to the returning exiles, "See, I am doing something new," forming a new people, "that they might announce my praise." Repentance is not something we do, but it allows the forgiving power of God to touch our lives and lead us along new paths.

The reading from John is a dramatic story of two trials. Jesus is put to the test by scribes and Pharisees (the usual suspects), who haul a woman caught in adultery before him and ask him whether he will approve the death penalty prescribed in the law of Moses (Deut 22:21; Ezek 16:38-40), so that they could perhaps brand him as a lawbreaker. The other trial is of a woman accused of a capital offense. Though powerful, this narrative is not found in the earliest and best manuscripts of John, and appears in other important manuscripts after Luke 21:38. Still, early Church authors, such as Papias (ca. A.D. 120) and the Syriac *Teaching of the Twelve Apostles* (third century), knew of such an incident, and Jerome included it in his translation, so it is canonical for Catholics. It may have been omitted in some early rigorist traditions because Jesus seems too "soft" on sin.

When challenged, Jesus does not respond but simply bends down and writes in the dust, then stands up with the ringing command, "Let the one among you who is without sin be the first to throw a stone at her." He then writes again on the ground and the accusers melt away, beginning with the elders, who, like the elders in the story of Susanna (Dan 13), probably brought the charge. Jesus' writing has spawned volumes of commentary, ranging from suggestions that it recalls Daniel's writing on the wall (Dan 5:24) to a proposal that Jesus first wrote Exodus 23:1, an edict against false witnesses, and a second time the sins of the accusers. A suasive suggestion is that Jesus' action attacks the accusers by alluding to Jeremiah 17:13: "all who forsake you shall be in disgrace; the rebels in the land shall be put to shame; they have forsaken the source of living waters [the Lord]" [NAB]. Whatever the best proposal, the attention shifts to Jesus and the woman standing alone. St. Augustine captures this scene poignantly: *relicti sunt duo miseria et misericordia* ("there are but two left, affliction and mercy"). Jesus asks the woman, "Woman, where are they [her accusers]? Has no one condemned you?" Her only words in the story are then, "No one, sir," and Jesus says, "Neither do I condemn you. Go, and from now on do not sin any more." Jesus' merciful compassion for the woman liberates her to turn her life toward a God of love.

This incident has inspired a wide variety of Christian art. The most striking is "Jesus and the Fallen Woman," by Lucas Cranach the Younger (ca. 1570), now exhibited, as is Rembrant's "Return of the Prodigal," in the Hermitage at St. Petersburg. At the front center of the painting are Jesus and the woman. Cranach captures that moment when Jesus turns toward the accusers and challenges those without sin to cast a stone. His expression is stern but troubled, and his right hand reaches out toward the woman. Most remarkable, the woman is not bowed to the ground in front of Jesus, as in much artwork, but is standing at his left. She is very young, with eyes closed, looking forlorn and resigned to her fate. Her head is inclined toward Jesus' shoulder, and her hand rests on his arm. Most striking as one follows the lines of the painting is that her right hand is entwined with the left hand of Jesus in a gesture of exquisite tenderness. The hands of mercy are joined to the hands of a suffering person facing execution.

When we gaze at the faces of Jesus and the woman, we might ask what face the Church presents to the world today. Often much preaching, especially in the area of sexual morality, is strident and condemnatory, with women often bearing the brunt of blame. Such preaching is a verbal equivalent of stone-throwing; yet Jesus holds the hand of a sinner. He does not claim that the woman did not sin; he simply does not condemn her for it and saves her from self-righteous accusers. Jesus and the young woman in Cranach's painting can be our guides through Lent and Paschaltide. With heads inclined toward Christ and hands intertwined with his, we can go forward as forgiven sinners, yet called to be companions of Jesus.

PRAYING WITH SCRIPTURE

- Pray the gospel quietly, putting yourself in the place of the different people—the accusers, the woman, Jesus.

- Check out your rock pile and think about those whom you were about to pelt with stones.

- Pray in community about how the Church can resist the death penalty.

Palm Sunday of the Lord's Passion

Procession with Palms: Luke 19:28-40
Readings: Isa 50:4-7; Ps 22; Phil 2:6-11; Luke 22:14–23:56
[or 23:1-49]

"Do not stay far from me,
for trouble is near,
and there is no one to help" (Ps 22:12).

BY THE CROSS, WEEPING

Each year Holy Week begins with a reenactment of Jesus entering Jerusalem amid shouts of praise. The week soon moves to his rejection, suffering, and death and concludes with the *preconium paschale*, the ringing proclamation that he has been raised. Each evangelist highlights different aspects. Luke adds to the acclamation "Blessed is the king who comes in the name of the Lord" the phrase "Peace in heaven and glory in the highest" (see Luke 2:14). During the passion Luke stresses that Jesus is a model of the innocent martyr. Pilate proclaims his innocence three times, as do Herod, one of the criminals at the cross, and the centurion. The Lukan Jesus prays for both Peter (22:32) and his persecutors (23:34) and remains a healer (22:51), teacher, and prophet. He is a model for all his followers who are unjustly executed. But just as this did not destroy Jesus, neither will it destroy those who witness to him.

During Holy Week the density of Scripture readings and the drama of the liturgies make preaching particularly challenging. It may be a time to imitate the early Church and reflect on Psalm 22, which resonates throughout the passion narratives, along with the other laments of Psalms 31, 38, and 69. Laments, the most frequent category among the psalms, begin with a cry to God expressing anguish, suffering, and abandonment, list reasons for the suffering, plead with God for release, and end with petition or praise. Laments give voice to suffering with the plaintive realization that alienation and suffering can be placed before God. The psalmist clings to God at that very moment of God's absence.

The earliest accounts of Jesus' suffering and death embody the theology of lament, and in the Synoptics the final words of Jesus are from laments. Prior even to a theology of atonement for sin or victory over death through resurrection, the early Church looked through the prism of the Old Testament and saw Jesus as the one who was abandoned by friends, mocked by enemies, and seemed forsaken by God. Jesus joins those whose agony smothers any sense of God's presence and who stand alone before the abyss of death, from Job (3:3-12), Jeremiah (20:15-18), through the servant of Isaiah 53, and down through history.

While the current liturgy stresses in Holy Week what God has done for us and points to the victory over death, the older liturgy, with the solemn chanting of Lamentations at Tenebrae and the somber observance of Good Friday, captured the sense of the horror of the unfolding events. In the United States today national rituals of lament have become an all too familiar celebration. Oklahoma City, Columbine, and countless memorials for the victims of the terrorist attack of September 11, 2001, enact ceremonies of grief as lives are snuffed out and futures shattered.

A few years ago I was giving a Scripture workshop on the Beatitudes. "Blessed are they who mourn" provided the occasion to reflect on the laments of the Old Testament. With the help of a sensitive young liturgist, we then put together an evening prayer of lament, modeled on the standard prayer that chose lament psalms and readings. In place of petitions we asked people to utter simple prayers such as "I grieve over . . ." or "I lament . . ." Each utterance was followed simply by prayerful silence—no requests for help, no expressed hope that it would come. Suppressed grief and frustration over the reign of evil in our world echoed through the chapel. There was a sense that Christ was praying in us during the waning hours of the day. Participants said it was one of the most moving and healing liturgies they had experienced.

The suffering of Jesus reminds us that his followers will also walk to many Calvarys. In a haunting lament our African-American brothers and sisters ask us if we were there "when they crucified my Lord." The passion narratives allow us to express abandonment and betrayal and to feel forsaken even by God, but assure us no one need tread the winepress alone. Jesus' final words in Mark repeat the beginning of Psalm 22, "My God, my God, why have you forsaken me?" In Luke Jesus dies with the words of another lament on his lips, "Father, into your hands I commend my spirit" (Ps 31:6). Arms are stretched out in abandonment, but eyes are raised up in trust. Behold the wood of the cross!

PRAYING WITH SCRIPTURE

- Pray over ways in which your family or parish may prepare rituals of lament.

- Pray quietly Psalms 22, 31, 38, and 69 in solidarity with those who most feel God's absence, and think of ways in which you might touch their lives.

- In prayer, walk with Simon of Cyrene who carries the cross of Jesus, and stand beside the women of Jerusalem who mourn and lament (Luke 23:26-31).

Easter Sunday: The Resurrection of the Lord

Readings: Acts 10:34a, 37-43; Ps 118; Col 3:1-4 or 1 Cor 5:6b-8; Luke 24:1-12

> **"Why do you seek the living one among the dead?"**
> **(Luke 24:5).**

A No-Nonsense Message!

The annual Easter proclamation reminds us of St. Augustine's hymn to Beauty (God): "ever ancient, ever new" (*Confessions*, 27). At the door of the tomb, the realm of death, the women hear an affirmation of life: "He is not here, but he has been raised." Echoing through the centuries, this is the foundation of Christian belief, and yet each evangelist scores it with different notes. The women who had followed Jesus from Galilee to the cross (Luke 8:1-3; 23:55) come to perform burial rites in love and devotion. They are greeted by two figures in white (the number of required legal witnesses), who announce the astounding news of the resurrection; then only Luke adds, "Why do you seek the living one among the dead?" The messengers then summon the women to an act of remembrance of Jesus' words that as suffering Son of Man, he would be handed over to crucifixion. Joyously remembering the words, the women announce all these things to "the eleven" and to the apostles, who were last mentioned at the Last Supper and who do not follow Jesus to the cross. They dismiss the women's announcement as "nonsense," and Peter, as in John 20:1-10, runs to the tomb, sees the burial clothes, and is amazed.

Distinct and powerful Lukan themes emerge. From his initial proclamation at Nazareth till his death, the Lukan Jesus is a prophet who brings God's word, but who will be rejected as were John and the prophets of old. His prophetic words are now fulfilled. Only after remembering these do the women become heralds of the resurrection. The enduring power of the words of Jesus reverberates through the Lukan resurrection appearances as the risen Jesus himself will break open the Scriptures for his followers (Luke 24:27). Resurrection faith today is not simply an affirmation of Jesus' victory over death and of his exaltation and enduring presence, but a summons to return to the words and deeds of Jesus in the Gospel.

Especially challenging are the apostles' disbelief and dismissal of the women's message. Some see it as first-century cultural bias against women's testimony and proclamation, which remains alive in the twenty-first century. Though Peter acts on the women's message, he is simply amazed at the empty tomb, but not yet a believer. In Luke's theology, not even the word of Jesus is enough to bring people to faith; they must have an experience of Christ's presence—which occurs in the following appearances to the two disappointed disciples on the way to Emmaus and the puzzled disciples in Jerusalem. Christian faith does not rest on an empty tomb, but on the continuing experience of the Risen One.

The resurrection proclamation to the women summons the disciples to remember not only the powerful words and deeds of Jesus but his suffering and death. Resurrection faith shares space with the horror of memories of a century when death seemed more regnant than life. The Vatican document "We Remember: A Reflection on the Holocaust" (March 16, 1998) calls on Christians to keep alive the scandal of its memory and to admit that in the past they "departed from the spirit of Christ and his Gospel," and concludes that the victims "from their graves, and the survivors through the vivid testimony of what they have suffered, have become a loud voice calling the attention of all humanity." Voices continue to be raised from the graves of victims of worldwide acts of genocide and other forms of lethal violence.

The message of resurrection, ever ancient, ever new, is that Christ is not "here" inhabiting the realm of the dead but has emptied death of its power. Catholics today are summoned to live, proclaim, and celebrate this victory by resisting all those forms of death and violence that saturate our culture. The women at the tomb remember the words of Jesus about suffering; their story, dismissed as nonsense, was that Jesus was raised up from the tomb, but only after descending into death's chamber. The flowers that adorn our homes and churches this Easter came from seeds that died and were transformed, as Christian life can flower through the mystery of the cross. The words from the Easter Sequence capture this beautifully: *Mors et vita duello conflixere mirando,* "Life and death are locked in wondrous struggle." The struggle endures, though ultimate victory is assured: *Dux vitae mortuus regnat vivus,* "Life's leader once dead reigns as the living one."

PRAYING WITH SCRIPTURE

- Place yourself beside the women at the tomb, puzzled, fearful, and hear again the Easter proclamation.

- Throughout Easter Day pray Psalm 118:1: "Give thanks to the LORD, for he is good; / for his mercy endures forever."

- While remembering the reign of death over the last century, reflect on how the Church may personify the "living one."

Second Sunday of Easter

Readings: Acts 5:12-16; Ps 118; Rev 1:9-11a, 12-13, 17-19;
John 20:19-31

"These are written
that you may come to believe" (John 20:31).

THE APOSTLE FROM MISSOURI

For those who have made the Spiritual Exercises of St. Ignatius (the full thirty days), the stress on "repetitions" initially seems tedious. Ignatius exhorts the retreatant to repeat and spend days or more on the same meditation, asking whether he or she feels consolation, desolation, or arrives at some new insight. The readings from Easter to Pentecost are similar. Continuous progression of a particular Gospel is not stressed, but repeating and reliving the paschal mystery of the death and resurrection of Jesus who continues to live in the Church are emphasized. Departing from the usual practice of Old Testament readings, the initial readings are from the Acts of the Apostles and provide vignettes of the initial flowering of the Church, a Church so led by the Holy Spirit that the Book of Acts has been called "the Acts of the Holy Spirit." The second readings in Cycle C present sections of the Book of Revelation (the Apocalypse), which assure a persecuted community of the reign of Christ in glory.

The Easter eve appearance to the disciples and to Thomas "a week later" bring the Easter octave to a close in all three cycles. One of the lost opportunities of the 1998 Sunday Lectionary revision was not including the appearance to Mary Magdalene (John 20:11-18) in the Easter readings, since it is integral to John's dramatic unfolding of the resurrection appearances. The gospel today tells how Jesus comes to the fearful disciples on Easter eve. He twice blesses them with the gift of peace, which in the Bible is the opposite of fear and fulfills his earlier promise that he will send the Paraclete (the advocate and consoler). They are to be the nucleus of a community of forgiveness which sends sin away (the literal meaning of "forgive") and which has power to hold back its destructive power.

The narrative of doubting Thomas, an early precursor of those living in the "Show Me" state, is unique among the resurrection appearances. When the other disciples repeat the same words of Mary Magdalene, "We have seen the Lord," Thomas scoffs and says that he will not believe without touching the wounds of Jesus. Suddenly Jesus appears and invites Thomas to do just what he demanded, saying, "Do not be unbelieving, but believe." Whether or not Thomas touched the wounds the text does not say, but he immediately answers, "My Lord and my God!"

Thomas, like many of the characters in John's Gospel, is representative or symbolic. In the story of the empty tomb, the Beloved Disciple, by arriving at the tomb first, is symbolic of the love that drives him to believe without actually seeing. Mary Magdalene symbolizes another form of love that continually seeks to embrace Jesus, only to be given a deeper challenge to her faith, namely, that Jesus will assume a new mode of presence, and she is to announce this to "his brothers." Thomas symbolizes those who are ready to believe in the resurrection, but on their own terms. Journeys to faith wind throughout John's Gospel (the Samaritan woman, the man born blind, and Martha of Bethany). These culminate in Jesus' words to Thomas, "Blessed are those who have not seen and have believed." The final verses before the appendix of John 21 are the evangelist's living legacy. The written words of his story are to lead people to faith and belief as powerfully as did the resurrection appearances, and such a journey will culminate in the gift of life.

Thomas, "the Twin," has many brothers and sisters in today's Church. Resurrection faith is crucial, but it is often on our own terms. Shortly after the Second Vatican Council, I was giving some lectures on the resurrection accounts, and a priest said to me: "Father, unless you can prove to me that Jesus rose from the dead, I cannot be a Christian." In my younger, more uncharitable days, I responded, "If I can prove to you that Jesus rose from the dead, you *should not* be a Christian." Resurrection remains that ever awesome and ever engaging mystery that invites us to faith but eludes certainty.

The image of Thomas standing before Jesus garbed not in the glowing white robe of popular art, but with gaping wounds, is powerful for the Church today. Rembert Weakland, O.S.B., when he was archbishop of Milwaukee, told young students inquiring about the deepest meaning of Catholicism to work one night a week in a soup kitchen and to attend Sunday Eucharist. The wounds of Christ mar his body as the broken and homeless shuffle forward for some meager sustenance, while breaking bread at liturgy reenacts his broken body on the cross.

Yet at both meals we are summoned to affirm, "My Lord and my God." Truly blessed are those who have not seen but have believed.

Praying with Scripture

- Gather with the disciples in fear and hear again the words of Christ, "Peace be with you."

- Pray over ways that gazing upon the wounds of Christ's mystical body can bring you to a deeper understanding of the Eucharist.

- Repeat in prayer the blessings that have come through your "believing."

Third Sunday of Easter

Readings: Acts 5:27-32, 40b-41; Ps 30; Rev 5:11-14; John 21:1-19

"Simon, son of John, do you love me?"(John 21:17).

A DIFFERENT CONCLAVE!

A papal conclave is among the most solemn events in Catholicism, replete with ancient rituals and a contemporary media feeding frenzy. Today's gospel presents a unique conclave of Jesus and his disciples—a fish fry by the Sea of Tiberias, which unfolds in two acts. In the first, the risen Jesus appears to his disciples and symbolizes their mission by a miraculous catch of fish (see Luke 5:1-11).

The Beloved Disciple is the first to recognize the figure on the shore as Jesus, another instance of the primacy of love. Yet Peter jumps into the water and drags a net ashore with 153 fish, a number that has funded two millennia of varying and wild speculation. For example, Cyril of Alexandria broke the number down with 100 signifying the fullness of the Gentiles, 50 the Jewish remnant, and 3 the Trinity. Rupert of Deutz identified the 100 with the married, the 50 with the widows, and 3 with the virgins [sic!]. Less fanciful, St. Jerome noted that Greek zoologists counted 153 species of fish.

Apart from number games, the catch of fish usually symbolizes the missionary outreach of the disciples (Mark 1:16-20; Matt 13:47). Since John uses exaggerated numbers to make a point (for example, John 2:6: 6 jugs of wine, each holding almost 30 gallons; Nicodemus arriving with 100 pounds of spices to anoint the body of Jesus), the main Johannine emphasis is on the bulging but not broken net, symbolizing the inclusive universality of the disciples' mission. Jesus prepares a meal of bread and fish for the disciples and, with "eucharistic" gestures, breaks it and gives it to them. The major thrust of this part of the story is that the risen Jesus comes again to commission his disciples to spread the Gospel and to assemble in eucharistic communion.

Act Two then narrows to a dialogue between Jesus and Simon. Having denied Jesus three times, Simon is then asked three times whether he loves Jesus, even becoming distressed after the first two protestations of love. Three times then Jesus commissions him, "Feed my lambs, tend my sheep, feed my sheep." Rather than giving an assurance of power and presence, as in the Matthean commissioning, Jesus predicts Peter's martyrdom. Only then does he say, simply, "Follow me."

At times interpreters have argued that the different words for love used here (*agapan* in the first two questions of Jesus, and *philein* in the final question and in all of Peter's answers) convey a movement from more emotional love to the deep love of friendship. Though John seems to use these terms interchangeably throughout his Gospel, the double use of *philein* in the final question and answer recalls Jesus' description of his disciples as "friends" when they do as he commands (15:15-16).

Today's gospel addresses the Church today. The community of disciples as a whole is involved in spreading the Gospel; the Beloved Disciple is a faithful witness whose love gives insight about Jesus, and Peter, the failed sinner, because of his love, is given pastoral care. Over the last millennium the Petrine ministry has been defined primarily in terms of Matthew 16:16-19, with its language of stability (rock), defensiveness (gates of hell shall not prevail), and the exercise of power (keys; bind and loose). As a new millennium unfolds, today's gospel could help to envision a "Johannine" Petrine ministry: a forgiven sinner, a leader in a community of friends chosen on the quality of love and given a primary mission of caring for and nurturing the vulnerable lambs and sheep in a world so harsh that it may lead to martyrdom.

PRAYING WITH SCRIPTURE

- Pray in gratitude for the manner in which the Church includes people of all cultural and national backgrounds.

- Pray that Church leaders may see their mission in light of Simon's seaside commission.

- Prayerfully realize that every ministry in the Church is ultimately one of nurture and love.

Fourth Sunday of Easter

Readings: Acts 13:14, 43-52; Ps 100; Rev 7:9, 14b-17; John 10:27-30

"His kindness endures forever, and his faithfulness, to all generations" (Ps 100:5).

CHOOSE LIFE!

Traditionally called "Good Shepherd Sunday," the gospel for each Lectionary cycle excerpts a segment of John 10:1-30. Proclamation and prayer require reflection on the complex of motifs found throughout the whole chapter. This year the gospel provides a fine linkage with last week's shepherding ministry of Peter, for whom Jesus is a model. Jesus twice calls himself the good shepherd, expressed by knowing the sheep and giving his life for them, in contrast with hirelings who neglect the sheep. The discourse concludes with a solemn affirmation by Jesus that his sheep hear his voice, that he knows them, and that his life given for their sake will bring them eternal life.

Life in its fullness and eternal life are major themes of John and are to be celebrated during this paschal season. Life is the prime characteristic of Jesus (1:4), and he comes to bring people eternal life (3:15-16). Such life does not begin after death, for the one who believes already has eternal life (3:36; 4:14) and has already passed from death into life (5:24). Eternal life cannot be taken away by death, but only by sin and unbelief, and Jesus is himself resurrection and life.

While most contemporary Christians have a strong hope in life beyond death, few would realize that they already possess "eternal life." In John's Gospel eternal life describes less duration or unending life than a quality or fullness of life. It is life with and for God which Jesus reveals and which begins when people through faith and love commit themselves to the kind and quality of life that Jesus embodies.

Still, not even the Johannine affirmation of the presence of eternal life amid everyday existence takes away fear of suffering and death.

Shortly before his untimely death (August 8, 1998), in *A Retreat with John the Evangelist: That You May Have Life*, Raymond E. Brown, S.S., taking the voice of the evangelist as retreat director, wrote: "The finality of death and the uncertainties it creates causes trembling also among those who have spent their lives professing Christ . . . [but] when confronted with the reality of the grave, all need to hear and proclaim the bold message that Jesus proclaims . . . 'everyone who believes in me shall never die at all.'"

Today the culture of death seems to envelop our lives at the very center of American life, from the killing fields of political, ethnic, and religious wars, through plagues of pandemics, and even to schoolyards. The promise of present and future eternal life seems fragile. Yet the Good Shepherd promises his flock and those other sheep not of his fold that no human life is meaningless or forgotten by God. Love, joy, and life await even those whose lives, barely unfolding, were snatched away, when "God will wipe away every tear from their eyes" (Rev 7:17).

PRAYING WITH SCRIPTURE

- Remember in prayer when your love, like that of the Beloved Disciple, led you to recognize Christ.

- Pray in gratitude for the different ways in which discipleship unfolds in the Church today.

- Recall a lost loved one, repeating often in prayer, "Everyone who believes in me shall never die at all."

Fifth Sunday of Easter

Readings: Acts 14:21-27; Ps 145; Rev 21:1-5a;
John 13:31-33a, 34-35

"Behold, God's dwelling is with the human race"
(Rev 21:3).

You Can Tell They Are Christians by What?

Vatican City, January 25, 2059. The recently elected pope, Victor IV, the former archbishop of Lusaka, Charles Tilyenji, who had taken the name of the first pope from Africa (St. Victor, 189–198), celebrated the traditional Mass for the Curia in St. Paul's Outside the Walls. It also marked the centenary of that day when Pope St. John XXIII had shocked the assembled cardinals by announcing his intent to convoke an ecumenical council.

In his address Pope Victor recalled the work of the Second Vatican Council and the hopes that it gave to the Church and the world. He then recounted the joy with which the Church celebrated the Great Jubilee and entered the new millennium. Sadly, he noted, recent world events had all but erased the joys and hopes that Vatican II called the Church to share with all peoples. The crop failures throughout the world had produced mass starvation, and the nuclear exchanges in the Middle East had depleted the world's oil supply, sparking a constant round of brush-fire wars and worldwide civil strife. In the United States the social fabric was torn apart as the gap widened between the super-wealthy and the desperate poor. Their political leaders of the last century never envisioned that a nation with more arms than people would devolve into internecine civil strife as devastating as the Civil War of the mid-nineteenth century.

The Holy Father expressed great sorrow that Catholics, far from being a light to the nations during these troubled times, had so often followed the path of violence and hatred. He mentioned that, when envisioning the Second Vatican Council, Pope John XXIII had been inspired by Jesus' prayer in John's Gospel that his followers "may be one even as we are one." Pope Victor then recalled that from his student days he had often prayed over the words of Jesus in John's Gospel: "I give you a new commandment: love one another. As I have loved you, so you also should love one another," and all people would recognize Jesus' disciples "if you have love one for another" (13:34-35). He questioned why the Church had so emphasized authority and doctrinal uniformity, while these words of Jesus, which sounded so simple but so essential, seemed at the margin of Church life.

Pope Victor then announced his plan to convene, not another formal ecumenical council, but a congress with representatives from the world college of bishops, religious, clergy, lay people, and other Christian leaders to explore how mutual, self-giving love might become the defining sign of Christ's followers.

A fantasy, a bad prophecy, perhaps, but today in 2004 we must ask if the kind of love that echoes through John's Gospel is a hallmark of Catholicism. God's love is the motive of the Incarnation. Jesus dies as one who lays down his life for a friend. The main disciple in John is not Peter but the Beloved Disciple. The words of today's gospel conclude the section on the Johannine footwashing, where Jesus symbolizes the kind of love the disciples are to have; he himself lives out that greater love that lays down one's life for a friend. The love of Mary of Magdala impels her to the tomb, where she meets her beloved, the risen Lord. Peter is entrusted with care for Jesus' flock only after a threefold profession of love.

The command of Jesus is both new and old. It repeats the precept of Leviticus 19:18 to love one's neighbor as one's self. What is new is that this love characterizes the new life inaugurated by Jesus and that it is proof of one's love for God (1 John 4:7). This love forsakes violence and is modeled on the self-offering of Jesus on the cross. It is not simply the love of feeling or passion, but as St. Ignatius reminded us, consists in mutual communication between persons and is manifest in deeds. As Dorothy Day states, such love is "a harsh and dreadful thing, [where] our very faith in love has been tried through fire," and she continues, "we cannot love God unless we love each other, and to love we must know each other. We know Him in the breaking of bread, and we know each other in the breaking of bread." The poet Ursula Le Guin captured the challenge of such love: "Love doesn't just sit there, like a stone; it has to be made, like bread, remade all the time, made new" (*The Lathe of Heaven*). At the beginning of a new millennium Christians are summoned to be breadmakers!

PRAYING WITH SCRIPTURE

- Repeat prayerfully and often today's gospel, along with 1 John 2:7-10; 3:10-11, 14-18; 4:7-11.

- Pray over how you might remake the loving relationships of your life.

- Pray over concrete ways that others will see love in deed as a defining characteristic of Christian communities.

Sixth Sunday of Easter

Readings: Acts 15:1-2, 22-29; Ps 67; Rev 21:10-14, 22-23;
John 14:23-29

> **"May the peoples praise you, O God;**
> **may all the peoples praise you!" (Ps 67:6).**

SPIRIT IN THE CHURCH

During the Easter season the readings celebrate the joy of the Resurrection, which culminates at Pentecost with the enduring gift of the Holy Spirit. The readings from the Acts of the Apostles recount the Spirit-directed spread of the Gospel and the almost idyllic life of the early Church, even amid suffering and persecution. We read these stories with a certain nostalgia for a simpler time when God was so tangibly present.

Yet today's first reading speaks of one of the most serious conflicts in the early Church. Often called the "Jerusalem council," Acts 15 tells of a landmark controversy between factions from the Jerusalem mother church and Paul and Barnabas over whether Gentiles must undergo circumcision in order to follow the Jewish Messiah, Jesus. The description of the division as "dissension" and "controversy" uses two of the strongest terms in antiquity for events that can destroy the fabric of a community.

While the first reading today depicts only the cause and the resolution of the controversy, the preceding weekday readings take us through the whole chapter. Acts 15 is at the mathematical midpoint of the book and represents a "changing of the guard," since the twelve apostles disappear from Acts, while the final chapters recount the career of Paul. The dispute arises after Paul comes to Jerusalem and recounts the conversion of the Gentiles. Converted Pharisees appear and claim that no one can become a Christian without circumcision. Before dismissing this as an arcane ritual, we should remember that first-century Jewish people saw this as an indispensable sign of God's covenant dating back to Abraham. The Books of Maccabees tell of people who died horrible deaths rather than abandon this practice. These Jewish converts may have cited a saying of Jesus, such as Matthew 5:18, that Jesus came not to abolish the law and prophets but to fulfill them, and that he himself was circumcised.

The dispute is resolved under the leadership of Peter, who recounts that God had called him to welcome the Gentiles (Acts 10), and by James, the leader of the Jewish-Christian Jerusalem church, who affirms Peter's experience and gives scriptural proof for the acceptance of Gentiles (Acts 15:14-18). Today's reading presents the letter that Paul and Barnabas were to carry ratifying their missionary practice of not requiring circumcision, while observing certain practices that provided the way to peaceful coexistence among Jewish and Gentile converts.

Today "dissent" and "dissenters" have become a shibboleth hurled at anyone who does not seem to toe a (selectively) orthodox line. Yet the Jerusalem council provides an example of the need to have faithful dissent. Peter's response to the division is that God revealed to him that the Gentiles received the Holy Spirit (Acts 15:8), and Paul and Barnabas recount "the signs and wonders that God had worked among the Gentiles through them" (15:12). These experiences lead the apostles and elders to conclude that "it seems good to the Holy Spirit and to us" to allow uncircumcised Gentiles into the family of faith. During this and every Easter season the Church is summoned to read the signs of the times, to see how God is working outside traditional structures of belief and practice and to discern new modes of living the Gospel. How can this happen? John's Gospel tells us: "The Advocate, the Holy Spirit, whom the Father will send in my name, will teach you everything and remind you of all that I told you" (14:26).

PRAYING WITH SCRIPTURE

- Pray that the Church may be attuned to those ways by which the Holy Spirit may lead us to new ways of living the Gospel.

- In prayer, think of those with whom you have serious disagreement, and reflect that God's Spirit may be working in them.

- Pray that the Church may continue to read the signs of the times as it faces contemporary challenges.

The Ascension of the Lord

Readings: Acts 1:1-11; Ps 47; Eph 1:17-23 or Heb 9:24-28; 10:19-23; Luke 24:46-53

**"You will receive power
when the Holy Spirit comes upon you" (Acts 1:8).**

DEPARTED, BUT NOT ABSENT

Only Luke recounts the Ascension, and it often seems a puzzling feast. A number of years ago I attended a children's liturgy in a vital parish. The priest told the children that he had bought a special gift to celebrate Ascension Thursday, and he asked what he had bought. Hands waved eagerly as the first platoon of responders suggested holy cards and pictures of Jesus. After many failed answers, one little tyke, with a beaming smile of assurance, suggested "a jack-in-the-box."

I do not remember the rest of the homily or how the priest brought the little ones to a deeper meaning of the feast, which Luke recounts twice, concluding the Gospel and inaugurating the Acts of the Apostles. It is a transition between the earthly and enduring presence of Jesus. At a time when Roman emperors were claiming divine power, Luke tells his community that the exalted Jesus is more powerful than any earthly power (see Eph 1:20-23). The Gospel presents fundamental themes of Luke. As in the other post-resurrection appearances, Jesus calls his disciples to return to the Scriptures ("It is written") to grapple with the mystery of his suffering and resurrection, so that "repentance, for the forgiveness of sins, would be preached in his name to all the nations." These final words provide an arch to the annunciation of the birth of John, who preached repentance and forgiveness (Luke 1:13-17) and to his canticle heralding the arrival of the daystar (Jesus), who announces forgiveness of sin and who gives light to those who sit in darkness (1:76-79).

The events following the resurrection of Jesus in the four Gospels should not be viewed as a sequence of historical happenings, but as different aspects of the one mystery of the resurrection and exaltation of Jesus. In John's Gospel Jesus ascends to the Father from the cross (John 19:30) and confers the Holy Spirit upon the disciples on the first Easter eve. While Luke places the ascension in Jerusalem, in Matthew Jesus departs from his disciples from a mountain in Galilee (Matt 28:16-20). Despite the differences, all the narratives communicate a sense of altered and transformed presence even amid the absence of the earthly Jesus. All also speak of a mission to continue the work of Jesus throughout the world and history.

The Lukan disciples are to be witnesses of Jesus' life and will be clothed in the Holy Spirit as they spread the Gospel to the ends of the earth. The ascension is about the exaltation of Jesus, not about his absence. We are not to stand "looking at the sky" (Acts 1:11) but at each other, at the Church which is his body (Eph 1:22-23), as a witness of forgiveness throughout history.

PRAYING WITH SCRIPTURE

- Luke's Gospel begins and ends on a note of great joy; in prayer, rejoice at the gifts the Gospel has brought to your life.

- Pray over how you can be a witness to the power of the risen Christ.

- The Letter to the Hebrews today speaks of "our confession that gives us hope." Pray over the ways in which your faith nurtures hope.

Seventh Sunday of Easter

Readings: Acts 7:55-60; Ps 97; Rev 22:12-14, 16-17, 20;
John 17:20-26

> **"Holy Father, I pray not only for them, but also for**
> **those who will believe in me through their word, so**
> **that they may all be one" (John 17:20-21).**

READING OF THE WILL

For almost four years *Tuesdays with Morrie* appeared on the bestseller list of the *New York Times.* It is a moving account by Mitch Albom of conversations with his dying mentor, Morrie Schwartz, who had earlier taught a course on "The Meaning of Life" and now unfolded even deeper meanings of life—his own and Mitch's.

Today's gospel reminds me of this. As his death approaches, Jesus speaks to his disciples of the deepest meaning of his life and of what faces them. John 17 has been called variously "The Testament of Jesus" or "Jesus' High Priestly or Intercessory Prayer." It is really both. The "testament" was a well-recognized convention at the time of Jesus (for example, farewell speeches of Moses in Deuteronomy and the *Testaments of the Twelve Patriarchs*). These comprise reflections on the meaning of life and parting advice to loved ones. Actually, all of John 13–17 comprises a testament, so it is easy to forget that the setting remains Jesus' final meal with those he now calls "friends." Earlier commentators have compared it to the eucharistic preface preceding the memorial of the passion.

Jesus' farewell discourse is the solemn language of prayer, especially John 17, which all three liturgical cycles excerpt on this Sunday. In the first part Jesus prays to the Father for his own glorification; in the second, that his disciples be unified and protected amid opposition from the world; and in today's reading the prayer is "not only for them, but also for those who will believe in me through their word" (John 17:20). The word "love" appears five times in four verses. Jesus prays that believers will be one, united by that very same love that unites him to the Father, and that this unity will be a sign that will bring "the world" to belief so that all may come to know God and the depth of God's love. God's glory will be found not in magnificent edifices or in structures of power, but in the love that unites Jesus' followers among themselves and to God. Through the disciples Jesus will continue to reveal God's name so that "the love with which you loved me may be in them and I in them" (John 17:26).

This final prayer for love provides an arch to the very beginning of the extended supper discourse, where Jesus, "having loved his own in the world, loved them to the end," and bequeaths to them a new commandment that they love one another as he has loved them. Now the disciples and the readers know just what "as I have loved you" means. Jesus goes to his death as a model of love, and through his death his followers will live in that very love which unites him to his Father. Later theology will adopt the category of sanctifying grace to describe such love.

Jesus' prayer for love and unity inspired Pope John XXIII to call a council to help break down divisions between contemporary followers of Jesus. In his recent encyclical *Ut Unum Sint* ("That They May Be One"), Pope John Paul II cites John 17:21-22 at least five times, stressing that the unity "which the Lord has bestowed on his Church and in which he wishes to embrace all people . . . stands at the very heart of Christ's mission" (no. 9), and urging common prayer to overcome the "painful reality" of Christian division (no. 22). The "Ecumenical Charter" issued on April 21, 2000, by the Conference of European Churches and the Council of European Bishops' Conferences, citing John 17:21, states, "If we are to be faithful to this prayer, we cannot be content with the present situation. Instead, aware of our guilt and ready to repent, we must strive to overcome the divisions still existing among us, so that together we may credibly proclaim the message of the Gospel among all people."

Though vital during the 1960s, the ecumenical movement today is beset by problems. Individual Churches are facing massive demographic and social changes that cause them to look inward, and religious divisions *within* ecclesial bodies are a scandal, while consuming great time and energy. Landmark agreed-upon statements have been the fruit of ecumenical dialogues, but often with little effect on Church life. The time is ripe for dramatic moves that may respond more faithfully to Christ's prayer that love characterize his followers and that they may be "one," so that "the world may believe that you sent me."

Morrie Schwartz's dying words to Mitch call him "my dear friend." Before his death Jesus calls his disciples "friends" if they do what he has commanded them (John 15:14-15), and his final words are a command to live in love and seek unity.

Praying with Scripture

- Pray with John 17 as a personal prayer for love and unity among Christians.

- Pray over ways that individually and as communities you might more often join in prayer with other Christians.

- As Pentecost approaches, pray that God's Spirit will inspire new ways of realizing the testament of Jesus.

Pentecost Sunday

Readings: Acts 2:1-11; Ps 104; Rom 8:8-17; John 14:15-16, 23b-26
(optional 1 Cor 12:3b-7, 12-13; John 20:19-23)

> **"The Advocate, the Holy Spirit whom the Father will
> send in my name, will teach you everything"
> (John 14:26).**

LIKE A STRONG DRIVING WIND!

Beginning in January 1977, the nation was captivated by the moving drama *Roots*, which told of the origin and earliest days of an African-American family. It enabled people to see their African-American brothers and sisters in a new light as a people with a noble heritage who had undergone the horrible sufferings of slavery and race hatred. It also fostered a concern for roots and study of family beginnings throughout the country. From our past we can learn what we have become, and perhaps what we should be.

The coming of the Holy Spirit at Pentecost and the subsequent stories of the growth and spread of Jesus' disciples throughout the Mediterranean world places us at the roots of our faith. Throughout history the Church has recalled the *vita apostolica*, the life of the early community, as both an ideal and paradigm for its life. On this Pentecost, as we approach "Ordinary Time," memories of this historical beginning and the early years of the Church can guide us today.

Prior to his ascension, the risen Jesus tells his disciples that they will "receive power when the Holy Spirit comes upon you," so that they will become witnesses "in Jerusalem, throughout Judea and Samaria, and to the ends of the earth" (Acts 1:8), which provides an overture to the expanding mission of the Church as it moves centrifugally outward from Jerusalem. Pentecost fulfills Jesus' promise as those gathered are baptized with the Holy Spirit and begin to witness the power of God, when, speaking their own language, they are understood by peoples representing the geographical boundaries of the known world. This

77

presents a reversal of the confusion of tongues at the tower of Babel (Gen 11:1-9) and anticipates the universal mission.

The dramatic coming of the Spirit does not cease with Pentecost. In Acts (often called "The Acts of the Holy Spirit"), the crucial break-throughs in the early Christian mission occur through the coming of the Spirit. The Holy Spirit comes upon the Samaritans at their conversion (8:17-18), and the long narrative of the "Pentecost of the Gentiles" (Acts 10) tells the story of Peter's "conversion" by realizing that "the gift of the Spirit had been poured out even on the Gentiles." At the critical council of Jerusalem (Acts 15), the Holy Spirit moves the community to admit Gentiles without the requirement of circumcision, which had functioned for a millennium as a sign of God's covenant and for which Jewish people had suffered martyrdom. The missionary journeys of Paul expand throughout the Mediterranean world under the power of the Spirit.

In Acts the Holy Spirit is the empowering and creative gift of God. Not only does the Spirit move the community outward in mission, it forms a Church that is inclusive. Gathered at Pentecost are not only the Twelve but women who were most likely those who followed Jesus in Galilee, were present at his death, and received first the resurrection proclamation. Mary, who was not mentioned by name after Luke 1–2 is present, and all receive the gift of the Spirit. Throughout Acts Luke pointedly adds women to the company of believers and to those persecuted for the faith, and later, Hellenistic women of means support the mission of Paul, while Priscilla and her husband Aquila are leaders and teachers in the Pauline communities.

Acts presents a favorable view of those who have not yet heard the Christian massage. The Spirit moves Philip to approach the Ethiopian court official who is reading Isaiah and immediately asks for baptism (Acts 8:26-40). Even prior to his conversion, Cornelius was "devout and God-fearing," gave alms to the Jewish people, and prayed "constantly." On the Hill of Mars in Athens, Paul sees an altar to an "Unknown God" and tells the Athenians that they were worshiping the God who is the creator and parent of the human race (Acts 17:16-34).

The Spirit shapes the inner life of the community. Luke offers an epitome of Christian life as a group joyfully gathered in prayer, devoting themselves to the teaching of the apostles and the breaking of the bread, and sharing of their goods and lives, so that economic and social distinctions are transcended (Acts 2:42-47 and 4:32-35). As the community moves forward in mission, persecution does not destroy it but stimulates it to further endeavor, and Christians speak constantly with courage and boldness. The joy with which the Gospel itself opens characterizes the life of the believers.

Pope John XXIII prayed that the Second Vatican Council would evoke a "new Pentecost" in the Church, and many new movements manifest the presence of the Spirit, such as the charismatic presence of Pope John Paul II, the growth of the Church in Africa, and the success of the RCIA. But for other movements, when people hear the wind rustling through the house, they quickly put storm windows on. The Spirit often seems to be identified with institutional centralization and power. Movements such as basic Christian communities are viewed with suspicion. Rather paradoxically, the fastest growing groups of Christians, especially in the "two-thirds world," are Pentecostals, whose theology and life reflect that of the Christian community in Acts, often literally. They are God-centered, stress transforming religious experience, appeal to the poor and disenfranchised, and thrive as small communities without centralized organization. As the Church celebrates its roots in the Pentecost event and moves through Ordinary Time, Acts provides a manual of discipleship for a Church in mission through the ages and reminds us that the Spirit works in wondrous and surprising ways.

PRAYING WITH SCRIPTURE

- Pray over times when you have felt the Holy Spirit enter your life, perhaps in surprising and disturbing ways.

- In prayer, ask the Holy Spirit to continue to break down those barriers that separate people and nations.

- Pray over the description of the Holy Spirit in the Pentecost Sequence as *consolator optime, dulcis hospes animae* ("of comforters the best, and the soul's most welcome guest").

[handwritten notes]
language barriers
customs - circumcision not necessary
    for Gentiles
mission - inclusivity in Church
economic barriers - shared their goods
social barriers - rich and poor belong

The Solemnity of the Most Holy Trinity

Readings: Prov 8:22-31; Ps 8; Rom 5:1-5; John 16:12-15

**"The love of God has been poured out into our hearts
through the Holy Spirit" (Rom 5:5).**

GOD FOR US!

Preachers often cringe when faced with a homily on Trinity Sunday. It is the only feast seemingly named after a doctrine, and many, of a certain generation, were taught that it was a *mysterium stricte dictum*, that is, totally beyond human comprehension and expressed only through analogy—hardly ready material for a June homily—St. Patrick and the shamrock notwithstanding. Belief in a triune God is fundamental to every Christian life rather than simply a topic for theological speculation. We begin every liturgy invoking the name of the Trinity and are sent forth with a blessing from Father, Son, and Spirit. God as "three Persons" shapes every aspect of our faith, from liturgy to concerns about social justice. The deepest meaning of the Trinity rooted in Scripture is not "God beyond us," but, in the words of the late Catherine Mowry LaCugna, "God for Us." Simply put, the Trinity expresses "the essential truth that the God who saves through Christ by the power of the Spirit lives eternally in the community of persons in love" (Catherine Mowry LaCugna, "Trinitarian Spirituality," in *The Collegeville Dictionary of Spirituality*, ed. Michael Downey [Collegeville, Minn.: The Liturgical Press, 1993]—highly recommended).

Today's readings, which speak of salvation effected through Christ and its effects, capture this insight beautifully. Romans 5 begins a major turning point in the letter. After a bleak picture of the human condition without God and a profound reflection on the need for God's grace by both Jew and Gentile, Paul begins a new section on the effects of God's free gift of salvation and justification in Jesus. Here, as in other places, he joins the action of Father, Son, and Spirit. We have peace, that is, the wholeness of a restored relationship with God, and stand in God's grace, which gives us a hope amid all difficulties. Paul hurries to the result: "the love of God [that is, the love God has for us] has been poured out into our hearts through the Holy Spirit." "Pouring" evokes the life-giving water of Isaiah 44:2-3: "Fear not, O Jacob, my servant, / the darling whom I have chosen. / I will pour out water upon the thirsty ground."

The gospel presents a section of Jesus' farewell discourse, in which he promises that the Spirit of truth will come to guide the disciples to all truth ("truth" in the sense of unveiling or revelation rather than verification). In John, the Spirit of truth promised after Jesus' departure is also called "Paraclete" ("Advocate" or "Counselor"—14:16, 26; 15:26; 16:7) as well as the "Holy Spirit" (14:26). The Spirit will effect in the lifetime of the community of disciples what Jesus did during his earthly ministry: guide them into truth, defend them in time of trial, and glorify (that is, make present) the Incarnate Word.

I fear these reflections may be guilty of my initial concern: making the Trinity more obscure. Yet the feast celebrates the nature of God existing for us and revealed to us. God is a creative and loving parent who pours out love by taking on the human condition even unto death and continues to live in our midst by forming a community of "beloved disciples" who live in imitation of the *koinōnia*, or intimate community of the divine Persons, and expresses this in love for others. We begin and end our liturgy invoking the Triune God as a symbol and mandate for a manner of life.

PRAYING WITH SCRIPTURE

- Pause frequently when making the sign of the cross, thinking of the love of God poured out into your heart.

- Pray over how the Trinity as a community of Persons should influence our relations with others.

- While listening to a running stream or the falling rain, repeat Paul's words, "the love of God has been poured out into our hearts through the Holy Spirit."

The Solemnity of the Most Holy Body
and Blood of Christ

Readings: Gen 14:18-20; Ps 110; 1 Cor 11:23-26; Luke 9:11b-17

"Do this in remembrance of me" (1 Cor 11:24).

YOU REALLY DON'T BELIEVE THAT, DO YOU?

Dating from the Middle Ages, this feast seems to duplicate the liturgy of Holy Thursday, but it also looks forward to the weekly eucharistic celebrations of "Ordinary Time." It is often celebrated with a festive procession, which can symbolize our need for the Eucharist on our own pilgrimage. Three themes permeate the readings: the Eucharist as blessing or praise of God (action of Melchizedek); as a memorial in which Jesus symbolically, through bread and wine, enacted his self-offering for others on the cross; and as food for the multitudes.

An important aspect of "the Catholic imagination" is the ability to hold many meanings of an event in creative tension rather than isolate a single interpretation. Eastern Orthodox liturgies have constantly stressed the Eucharist as blessing or praise of God expressed in solemn ritual and song. Catholics for centuries emphasized "the Holy Sacrifice of the Mass," while after Vatican II, liturgical changes accentuated the meal, symbolized by a simple altar table with the celebrant as presider or host of the meal. Each of these valid interpretations can be distorted through exaggeration. The Eucharist is truly a banquet for multitudes (Luke), but it is also a memorial of the last meal of a condemned person; it is a reenactment of Christ's sacrificial self-giving, but this can lead to a privatistic appropriation by individual believers.

Sadly, today, exaggerated stress on one meaning has created not simply diversity but at times scandalous divisions among Catholics, as instanced by the groundless attacks by Mother Angelica and other ultra-conservative authors on Cardinal Roger Mahony's pastoral letter "'Gather Faithfully Together': A Guide for Sunday Mass" (September 4, 1997). Often this devotion has encouraged an exaggerated physicalism about Christ's presence in the Eucharist (remember the stories of hosts dripping blood). Though from a learned Catholic philosopher, the following view is theologically problematic: "It . . . has not ceased to amaze me that Almighty God suffers me to touch him, move him, eat him. Imagine! When I move my hand to my mouth with the Host, I move God through space" (Peter Kreeft, *Fundamentals of the Faith* [San Francisco: Ignatius Press, 1988]). The presence of Christ is "real" and "substantial," but not physical (*Catechism of Catholic Church*, nos. 1373-79). Theologically, the Real Presence affirms the presence of the glorified Christ. "Thus we do not physically touch Christ in the Eucharist, nor can His body suffer violence when the species are desecrated or burned" *(New Catholic Encyclopedia*, 5:606). The Church affirms other forms of "real presence": "in his word, in his Church's prayer, in the poor, the sick and the imprisoned, in the sacraments, in the sacrifice of the Mass, in the minister" (*Catechism of the Catholic Church*, no. 1373). The Eucharist is the *focus* of real presence rather than its sole locus.

The feast of the Body and Blood of Christ reminds us also that we share in the communion of Christ's body and blood. Over thirty-five years ago I was traveling from Germany to Israel to study modern Hebrew. During a stopover in Lebanon, I struck up a conversation with a young Moslem student at breakfast. He began to question me about Catholic teaching on the Eucharist. Freshly minted from theology and armed with the earliest and latest Scholastic distinctions, I thought I was responding to his concerns about our belief in the Real Presence. None of my responses seemed to address his deepest concerns, until finally I said, "What is your most basic problem with what Catholics believe about the Eucharist?" He thought for a moment and said, "Well, if they really believed they were receiving the body and blood of Christ together on Sunday, would they treat each other the way they do?" Not a bad thought for the feast of Corpus Christi.

PRAYING WITH SCRIPTURE

- In those quiet moments after receiving the body and blood of Christ, pray for greater unity and mutual understanding among Catholics.

- The Eucharist is food for a pilgrim journey. Pray for a greater experience of this during "Ordinary Time."

- Read prayerfully from the Sunday liturgy the Sequence *Lauda Sion Salvatorem* ("Laud, O Zion, your salvation"), written by St. Thomas Aquinas and used on this feast.

Twelfth Sunday in Ordinary Time

Readings: Zech 12:10-11; 13:1; Ps 63; Gal 3:26-29; Luke 9:18-24

"But who do you say that I am?" (Luke 9:20).

At the Crossroad

Today begins "Ordinary Time," which extends until Advent. Recently, during a course on John's Gospel, a seminarian who was born after the Second Vatican Council, while we were discussing the Holy Spirit, suggested that we call these Sundays "the Sundays after Pentecost," which, he commented, was the custom for most other Christian bodies. He felt that they were not "ordinary," but a continuing journey guided by the Holy Spirit. In reminding him that this was once our centuries-old custom, I realized that some liturgical changes have dimmed the splendor of tradition.

The readings today furnish a powerful overture to our journey in the Spirit, as they function in Luke's Gospel as the prelude to Jesus' journey to Jerusalem. In the first reading Zechariah speaks of the outpouring of a spirit of grace and petition, when people will "look on him whom they have pierced," which has now been actualized in the crucifixion of Jesus. In the second reading Paul invokes an early baptismal formula that speaks of our adoption as sons and daughters of God in baptism, through which we have "clothed ourselves with Christ" and live a transformed existence that breaks down the barriers of gender, race, and social status. The gospel poses to us at the outset of our renewed journey a question ever old and ever new: "Who do you say that I [Jesus] am?" Our tour through Luke's narrative provides way stations as we strive to answer this question.

Though "the confession of Peter" is recounted in all three Synoptic Gospels, each evangelist weaves a different tapestry. Mark stresses the shock of Jesus' prediction of suffering and death and Peter's failure to accept it. Matthew elaborates Peter's confession into a church-founding story, while Luke directs the prediction and the sayings that follow to

84

all would-be followers of Jesus. Most dramatically, Luke says that every follower of Jesus must take up his cross *daily*—clearly not a reference to literal martyrdom. Nor is this invitation a summons to Christian "masochism" or a stoic, teeth-grinding submission to suffering. Self-denial, literally saying no to self, is a commitment to counter those things in our lives and personality that preclude saying yes to others. Daily cross-bearing is always "for my [Jesus'] sake"; it is a way of giving testimony that the example of Jesus forms a life of discipleship. Such cross-bearing takes place every time parents care for a disabled child or when Alzheimer's disease strikes a couple; it is visible in the loving care that health-care workers give to victims of the most debilitating diseases, and in prophetic and costly stances against violence and injustice. Through God's grace such "denial of self" is paradoxically the prelude to fullness of life (saving one's life).

A generation ago the theologian and martyr Dietrich Bonhoeffer spelled out the meaning of such discipleship when he contrasted the "cheap grace" offered by mainline Churches with the "costly grace" of true discipleship. The former he described in vivid terms: "Cheap grace means grace sold on the market like cheapjack's wares. The sacraments, the forgiveness of sin, and the consolations of religion are thrown away at cut rate prices. . . . Cheap grace is grace without discipleship, and grace without the cross, grace without Jesus Christ, living and incarnate." In contrast, "Costly grace is the gospel which must be sought again and again, the gift which must be asked for, the door at which a man must knock. Such grace is costly because it calls us to follow, and it is grace because it calls us to follow Jesus Christ. It is costly because it costs his life and it is grace because it gives a man the only true life. It is costly because it condemns sin and grace because it justifies the sinner. Above all, it is costly because it cost God the life of his Son" (*The Cost of Discipleship* [New York: Macmillan, 1959], pp. 45–53). Often today the Church dispenses such "cheap grace" when limpid apologies, with little real prospect of remedy for problems, substitute for true confession of sin and a "firm purpose of amendment."

Paul's vision of baptismal unity in Galatians offers a program for costly discipleship today. Our world is racked by ethnic and religious divisions, social injustice grows unchecked, and women continue to suffer injustice and violence in all spheres of life. Sadly, Christians are often no better at confronting these evils than their non-believing counterparts. Satisfying marketed needs rather than saying no to self drives advertising and the mercantile economy. Racism, often more covert and thus more dangerous, is the subtext of much political rhetoric, and one sad result of terrorist attacks is the return of a recycled nativism that sees people of different color and culture as a threat. As we follow the steps of Jesus through the Gospel of Luke, we may realize that the discipleship to which he summons his followers is directly counter to the supposed values that shape much of our world. Yet Jesus promises to those who say no to these and who witness to his life and values that they will find their true lives.

PRAYING WITH SCRIPTURE

- In prayer, reflect often how you would answer the questions of Jesus, "Who do the crowds say that I am? . . . But who do you say that I am?"

- Pray over those false values that threaten your true self, while asking God's grace to seek true life.

- Pray how you might "clothe yourself with Christ."

Thirteenth Sunday in Ordinary Time

Readings: 1 Kgs 19:16b, 19-21; Ps 16; Gal 5:1, 13-18; Luke 9:51-62

"I will follow you wherever you go" (Luke 9:57).

SHAPING UP FOR THE REIGN OF GOD!

I will never forget my visit to Africa over twenty years ago. I arrived in Nairobi after a long journey and received a kind welcome at the airport, only to be sent on a perilous journey to the GABA Institute in Eldoret. I traveled along the winding roads of the Great Rift Valley in a *matatu*, a local taxi, with drivers more suited to Indianapolis than mountain roads. My most vivid impression, though, was of great numbers of people walking along the side of the road. It became for me a metaphor of a continent on the move. Now I realize that even in the motorized West, our lives consist of different kinds of journeys.

Today's gospel inaugurates the long Lukan narrative of Jesus' journey from Galilee to Jerusalem, where he will be taken up (both on the cross and to God). It is the theological centerpiece of Luke's Gospel, containing his major themes (mercy, compassion, prayer and concern for the marginal), as well as memorable treasures of the Gospel (the parables of the Good Samaritan, the Prodigal Son, the Widow and the Judge). The beginning of the journey sets the tone: Jesus will be the rejected prophet who equally rejects violent response to rebuffs. He then spells out the demands of discipleship for those who would follow him: itinerant lifestyle, neglect of the most sacred family obligations (burial of a father), and an instant commitment that surpasses care for loved ones. The disciple is to imitate the prophetic vocation of Jesus.

The journey begins on an ominous note. Jesus sends his disciples to a Samaritan village to "prepare for his reception there." When the Samaritans hear that he is on his way to Jerusalem, they roll up the welcome mat. At this time the hatred between Jews and Samaritans was especially bitter, though they both followed the Torah of Moses; in John 4:7-9 the Samaritan woman is surprised that Jesus, "a Jew," even asks her for a drink. When the disciples James and John (called elsewhere "sons of thunder") saw this, they suggested to Jesus that they call down "fire from heaven to consume them," reminiscent perhaps of the destruction of Sodom for its violation of the ancient conventions of hospitality (Gen 19:1-29). Jesus immediately "turned and rebuked them," a term used when Jesus rebuke[s] demons. More importantly, early in the travel narrative, when Jesus wants to illustrate love of neighbor, he tells a parable of a Samaritan who showed compassion to a dying man (Luke 10:29-37), and near the end of the journey he points to a healed Samaritan leper as a model of gratitude to God (17:11-19). While the disciples seek vengeance on enemies, Jesus points to them as models of discipleship.

Jesus' challenging call to radical discipleship has rarely been followed literally, even in the Acts of the Apostles, and today is most often the topic of the lives of saints. Yet the challenges of Jesus can still speak to all of us. To begin a journey with Jesus is to place the demands of God's reign at the center of our lives, and in areas as central to our culture as was familial obligation at the time of Jesus. We must balance strong commitments to our beliefs with forsaking angry response to those who reject our values. We must realize that those we call enemies may bring messages of God's love and power. In individualistic and materialistic America, our choices in life can be dominated by a desire to preserve a destructive lifestyle. Jesus may not ask today that we leave our homes but that we think of those who have none; God's reign today does not require that we leave the dead unburied but rather think of how those already born may have a chance in life.

PRAYING WITH SCRIPTURE

• Reflect prayerfully over those times when you have prepared the way for God to enter others' lives.

• What does it mean today to be "fit for the kingdom of God" as you reflect on your journey with Christ?

• In moments of rejection, when we feel like calling down fire on someone, think of Jesus turning to rebuke us.

Fourteenth Sunday in Ordinary Time

Readings: Isa 66:10-14c; Ps 66; Gal 6:14-18; Luke 10:1-12, 17-20

**"As a mother comforts her child,
so will I comfort you" (Isa 66:13).**

ON THE ROAD

During the summer months people are on the move as luggage-laden cars inch along packed highways or hordes of people head for airports, all with the hope of some restful change from ordinary life. Today's readings picture people on the move, but for very different reasons. The reading from Isaiah concludes that book with the hope that the returning exiles will again "nurse with delight / at her [Jerusalem's] abundant breasts," which is followed by the gathering of "nations of every language" before Israel's God (66:18). In the gospel Jesus sends seventy-two followers on a journey to proclaim peace, bring healing, and announce that God's kingdom is at hand.

While all the Synoptic Gospels include a mission of the Twelve, only Luke adds a second mission of the seventy-two (or in many manuscripts the seventy). The numbers are symbolic, perhaps, of the seventy-two nations of the world in Genesis 10 or of the seventy elders whom Moses chooses to be assistants (Exod 24:1). This second Lukan mission prepares the way for the universal mission of the Church in Acts and repeats the motif from Isaiah that God's goodness is inclusive of all peoples.

The Lukan missionaries are to travel light, with a deep trust in God and in those who will receive them. Their first words whenever they enter a house are "Peace to this household," and if a person characterized by peace welcomes them, God's peace will rest on that house. Peace is the biblical *shalôm*, "wholeness" or "security," the result of a right relationship with God and neighbor (see, Isa 32:17: "Justice will bring about peace; / right will produce calm and security"). The God of Isaiah promises the returning exiles: "I will spread [peace] over Jerusalem like a river" (NAB translates as "prosperity over," but the original Hebrew is *shalôm*). In Isaiah, God who brings peace is compared to a mother cradling and comforting a child (also Isa 45:15).

Yet another voice hovers behind Isaiah's vision of peace and the gospel message. Jesus foretells rejection of the traveling missionaries and demonic opposition, and through the centuries Isaiah's Jerusalem has most often been a mother mourning for her children. (Hardly a week goes by there without a cycle of murder and reprisals.) Complete peace with God and within the human family may never unfold in human history, but it remains both a mandate and an ideal for which Christians in mission will continue to suffer. In urging dialogue to break down those religious barriers that have fostered wars of religion, Pope John Paul II wrote: "The name of the one God must become increasingly what it is: a name of peace and a summons to peace" ("At the Beginning of the Third Millennium," no. 55). Wherever they travel, Christians must first say, "Peace to this household."

PRAYING WITH SCRIPTURE

- Vatican II used the image of "the pilgrim Church," a Church on the move. Prayerfully reflect on its significance.

- In prayer, ask God to make of you a messenger of peace.

- In prayer, think how every believer is called also to be a person in mission.

Fifteenth Sunday in Ordinary Time

Readings: Deut 30:10-14; Ps 69 or Ps 19; Col 1:15-20;
Luke 10:25-37

"Go and do likewise" (Luke 10:37).

A JOURNEY INTERRUPTED

Very few parables of Jesus have had the impact of the story of the Samaritan who stops and helps an injured man on the desolate road to Jericho. The Good Samaritan has been portrayed in art in the Lancet Window at Chartres and by Bassano, Giordano, and Rembrandt. Hospitals and health-care systems have taken its name. It is a byword for anyone helping another in need, and one contemporary firm even markets Good Samaritan Healing Ointment, touted as the best ointment on the market for cuts, scrapes, and even diaper rash! Yet the parable is more profound, more than a startling example of compassionate help.

The narrative begins with a lawyer testing Jesus about the requirements for eternal life. Jesus turns the question back on him, and he correctly articulates the two great commands of the Jewish law: total love of God and love of neighbor as one's self. The lawyer then has a follow-up question and asks, "Who is my neighbor?" This evokes the parable, which does not answer the lawyer's question but tells him what it is to be neighbor and, subtly, who is neighbor.

The story describes a man beaten, robbed, and left half dead on the Jericho road. All identifying characteristics are gone; we do not know whether he is rich or poor, Jew or Samaritan. Three travelers come down the road. The first, a priest, arrives "by chance" (NAB: "happened"), sees him, and walks past, as does the second, a Levite. Too often we can interpret this as a bit of anti-Jewish polemic, but if the priest and Levite were going to Jericho to perform religious duties, any contact with a corpse would have made them unclean. They are good people caught in a dilemma. Next comes a Samaritan. Given the intense hatred at the time of Jesus between Jews and Samaritans (see

John 4:9; 8:48), Jesus' hearers may have expected the Samaritan to finish the man off. Yet the rhythm of seeing and passing by is broken by the explosive Greek verb *esplagchnisthē,* he was "moved with compassion." Only then does the Samaritan enter the world of the injured man with saving help. Luke combines seeing and compassion when Jesus sees and has compassion on the widow at Nain (7:13) and when the father welcomes home the returning prodigal (15:20). Compassion is the divine quality that, when present in human beings, enables them to feel deeply the suffering of others and move from the world of observer to the world of helper.

Like all parables, this story has multiple meanings. Most shocking in the parable, though, is not that someone stopped. It would be a story of compassion if a Jewish lay person stopped. The parable forces us as readers to put together "good" and "Samaritan." The outsider provides the model of love of neighbor; the apostate fulfills the law. We might also put ourselves battered in the ditch and ask if we are ready to be helped by those whom we would classify as outsiders. Who today teaches us and enacts for us the meaning of love of God and neighbor? The lawyer grudgingly answers, "The one who treated him with mercy." Can we live out this answer?

PRAYING WITH SCRIPTURE

- Pray with the parable of the Good Samaritan, identifying with each of the characters. What thoughts and feelings arise?

- Ask God for a compassionate vision for suffering people whose paths you may cross.

- Pray in gratitude for those times when "Samaritans" have stopped to help.

Sixteenth Sunday in Ordinary Time

Readings: Gen 18:1-10a; Ps 15; Col 1:24-28; Luke 10:38-42

"He waited on them under the tree while they ate" (Gen 18:8).

PUTTING OUT THE WELCOME MAT

Recently the Jesuits were given pastoral care of St. Patrick's Parish in Oakland, California, a small but spirited parish composed mainly of African-Americans and Hispanics, a community that radiates hospitality. One of the great "saints" of the parish is Mother Dumas, age 98, matriarch of a large family extending through five generations. Her daughter Ophelia is one of the official greeters, and visitors to the parish are seated next to Mother Dumas as she sits before the Lord in the front pew. Holiness is contagious.

I thought of this while reading today's readings. They are all about hospitality. Abraham and Sarah welcome into their tent three strangers, wash their feet, and prepare a meal. For this they are blessed with an heir. Luke tells of Martha "welcoming" Jesus into her home. "Welcome" is a somewhat pallid translation of one of the most important concepts in early Christianity. It suggests receiving someone as a guest, spending time with them, sharing a life with them. The spread of Christianity was due to the welcome given to traveling missionaries, and Paul urges that Christians welcome those of other views and practices (Rom 14:1).

Yet this somewhat idyllic scene changes. Martha's sister Mary sits at the feet of the Lord just "listening to him speak" (original Greek: "listening to his word"). Martha, "burdened with much serving," complains, and surprisingly Jesus chides her for her worrisome anxiety and says that Mary has chosen the better part (or as many translations say, "a good" part), which shall not be taken away.

This story has produced a rich feast of interpretations. In much of Church history it exalts the contemplative life (Mary) over the active life (Martha). In thirty years of teaching I have rarely found a woman or man who does not identify with Martha, even though one woman described her as a "whiny workaholic." Some contemporary feminist scholars see Jesus' remark as a disparagement of the diaconal ministry of women. But there are other options.

Coming on the heels of the Good Samaritan, the narrative is parabolic and meant to be shocking. Having just heard Jesus tell the story of someone who goes the extra mile to help a suffering neighbor, we would expect Jesus to urge Mary to help Martha. The key may be in the description of Mary sitting at the Lord's feet, a technical term for discipleship (Acts 22:3), and her action of hearing his word recalls the group whom Luke highlights as "ministers of the word" (1:2). Mary's ministry of the word is defended in the face of traditional gender roles. But the point of this parabolic narrative, when coupled with the Good Samaritan, is that love of God and of neighbor requires both compassionate entry into the world of the neighbor and silent sitting in God's presence. While highlighting Mary, in the larger context the story does not reject Martha. The returning Jesus will himself perform the work of Martha (Luke 12:37). Both Mary and Martha are saints, and a welcoming Church cannot thrive without Ophelia and Mother Dumas.

PRAYING WITH SCRIPTURE

- Imitate Mary by quietly sitting in the presence of Christ.

- Pray for those countless people who welcome the marginal and homeless and prepare food for them.

- I have heard Catholic churches often described as "formal" or "cold." Pray over ways that your parish or community may be more welcoming.

Seventeenth Sunday in Ordinary Time

Readings: Gen 18:20-32; Ps 138; Col 2:12-14; Luke 11:1-13

> **"When I called you answered me;
> you built up strength within me" (Ps 138:3).**

Knocking, Knocking at the Midnight Door

Following the narrative of one praised for quietly sitting in the Lord's presence, this Sunday's readings focus on the need to voice one's concerns to God in prayer and on how we should pray. The specific instructions are prefaced by Luke's version of the Lord's Prayer. Luke's version is both shorter and more ordered to everyday life than Matthew's strongly eschatological version (6:9-13). The prayer echoes the Jewish prayer called the *Qaddish:* "Exalted and hallowed be his great name. . . . May he establish his kingdom in your lifetime and in your days." In Luke the disciples are to pray not simply for daily bread but that it come "each day," and that God's forgiveness of sin be measured by their willingness to forgive debts. They ask God's protection from "testing," which is both the final judgment and the trials that will accompany their mission of evangelization.

The following somewhat humorous parable stresses the need for a brash and tenacious attitude in prayer. A man and his family are in bed in their one-room dwelling when a friend comes pounding on the door with a crisis. A friend of his has arrived in the middle of the night, and customs of hospitality demand that he fix him a meal, but the larder is empty. The sleeping man envisions rousting the whole family and lifting the unwieldy latch from the door. One point of the parable is not that God is sleeping when we pray, but that when a crisis is present, we should be willing to cause a divine ruckus. Abraham is a model of "bothering" God with a tenacious persistence, and today I think of the candid prayers of Tevye in *Fiddler on the Roof* or of St. Teresa of Avila's advice to pray with a "holy daring."

The following sayings address what for most Christians is the utter mystery of prayer: "Ask and you will receive; seek and you will find." We have all prayed constantly for some favor to be granted or for a sick or dying friend, only to be disappointed. I think some members of Luke's community felt the same way, for Jesus then speaks of how a loving father listens to the needs of his children. If he knows how to give good gifts, no matter what the request, then how much more will the heavenly Father give the Holy Spirit. For Luke, the Spirit is the ultimate and greatest gift that overshadows Mary and empowers the Church. Seemingly unanswered prayers are answered in surprising ways and in God's own good time. Often we become what we pray for—prayers for peace create people of peace; prayers for healing form hearts of compassion. The emptiness of seemingly unanswered prayers is filled by the gift of God's Spirit.

PRAYING WITH SCRIPTURE

- As you pray for God's forgiveness, think of those whom you should forgive.

- Prayerfully reflect how "unanswered" prayers have often been granted in surprising ways.

- Reflect on how the practice of prayer has opened you to God's Spirit.

Eighteenth Sunday in Ordinary Time

Readings: Eccl 1:2; 2:21-23; Ps 90; Col 3:1-5, 9-11; Luke 12:13-21

"What shall I do?" (Luke 12:17).

MANAGING YOUR PORTFOLIO

The host of a morning news program was interviewing a writer from *Forbes* magazine who was lamenting the financial losses suffered by various dot.com billionaires. He said that one person's fortune had fallen to a mere $170 million, and another had only a billion left. I could barely hold back my tears. What a change when I approached the Sunday readings. "Vanity of vanities," says dour Qoheleth, who goes on to recount the perils of wealth, while Jesus tells a parable about the danger of greed and the fragility of wealth. Hardly grist for summer vacation, prayer, and preaching!

Luke begins with an all-too-familiar fight over an inheritance, which Jesus is asked to adjudicate. Jesus refuses but warns against greed by recounting a parable that illustrates that one's life does not consist of possessions. Greed (literally in Greek, *pleonexia*, desiring more and more) is one of the most pilloried vices in antiquity, called by Diodorus Siculus "the metropolis of all evil." Paul calls it idolatry, since the desire for wealth begins to take over one's life (Col 3:5).

The parable begins on a positive note. A rich man's land produced a bountiful harvest, usually a sign of God's blessing. The parable then switches to a long soliloquy in which the man ponders his future. He attempts to secure this future by building bigger barns, storing the grain and other goods, so he can sit back and say, "You have so many good things stored up for many years, rest, eat, drink, be merry!" Suddenly the voice of God thunders, "You fool" (using language forbidden to humans—Matt 5:21-22), "this night your life will be demanded of you." Luke's readers would have seen horror in the death of the rich man. He dies alone rather than surrounded by family. In his lifetime he talked to himself about his wealth, and at his death he dies alone surrounded only by his wealth. Jesus then utters the ominous warning that "thus will it be for all who store up treasure for themselves but are not rich in what matters to God."

A rather harsh God emerges from this parable. Why did the rich man merit such condemnation? Some have suggested that he wanted to corner the market on grain and drive prices up. More likely he has turned his back on his Jewish heritage, where Torah demands that gleanings from a harvest be left for the poor, the widow, the orphan, and the immigrant (Lev 19:9-10; 23:22; Deut 24:21). Having rejected God's word, God's voice condemns him.

Today's readings present a special challenge to prosperous America. The gap between rich and poor widens; bigger homes, bigger cars ("What would Jesus drive?"), and bigger home entertainment centers are the modern equivalence of the bigger barns. How shall Christians today become "rich in what matters to God?" Skip *The Prayer of Jabez*, and take Luke's Gospel to the beach.

PRAYING WITH SCRIPTURE

- Reflect with Qoheleth on the "vanities" that can take over our lives (first reading).

- Pray that civil leaders may be more attuned to the needs of the poor and the vulnerable.

- Pray over ways that young people may be instilled with true values in a consumerist society.

Nineteenth Sunday in Ordinary Time

Readings: Wis 18:6-9; Ps 33; Heb 11:1-2, 8-19; Luke 12:32-48

**"May your kindness, O LORD, be upon us
who have put our hope in you" (Ps 33:22).**

FINDING THE TREASURE

This Sunday's gospel makes for difficult reading during the dog days of summer. It speaks of things we would rather gently put aside: simple lifestyle, almsgiving, readiness for the return of the Lord, faithful use of the time given us, and warnings of punishment. The initial verses of the gospel (vv. 32-34) are actually the Lukan conclusion to the long section on proper use of possessions that began with last week's gospel. In the section omitted from the Lectionary (Luke 12:22-31), Jesus proclaims freedom from material anxieties and a radical trust in God, who cares for the birds of the air and the lilies of the field (see Matt 6:25-34), and concludes with an exhortation to seek real treasures with God, for "where your treasure is, there also will your heart be." The heart is the biblical center of a person's being and designates what is most important. Luke here also reflects Jewish wisdom teaching, where true treasures are "righteousness which delivers from death" (Prov 10:2) [author's translation] and wisdom that fills a person's house with treasure (Prov 24:3-4).

The gospel, addressed no longer to the crowds but to Jesus' disciples, continues with two allegories on the need for responsible stewardship by Jesus' disciples (reminiscent of the "two ways" theology of Deuteronomy 30:11-20). A master is away at a wedding feast (an image of Jesus' absence as the community awaits the messianic banquet). He returns and finds that the servants have been vigilant during his absence. He immediately assumes the role of servant and prepares dinner for them. The second allegory is a warning about abusing the time before the return of Jesus. The servant who is now explicitly in charge of the master's property does not care for the community but for himself and resorts to violence. He will be punished severely (literally "cut off" from the community) and placed with the unbelievers. Two ways emerge for church leaders of Luke's day and for our time. A heart transformed and freedom from care and from the desire for wealth and power are prerequisites for responsible leadership in the community. Misuse of an office for one's own advantage and abuse of others will bring about severe punishment.

The long praise of the faith of Abraham and of "the ancients" from Hebrews (second reading) provides the basis for faithful discipleship and leadership. Abraham began his pilgrim journey in faith and was even ready to sacrifice his future in the person of his son Isaac. The ancients (most likely a reference to those wandering in the wilderness after the Exodus) did not look to the past but lived out of God's promises. Future hope rather than present trials shaped their lives, for "faith is the realization of what is hoped for and evidence of things not seen" (Heb 11:1).

As I am writing these lines, the Church is reeling both from sexual crimes of clergy and lack of episcopal leadership, vividly shown by the resignation of Cardinal Bernard Law of Boston. It is a time when faith is tested, and people must ask themselves where their treasure is. Yet it is a time when Jesus will come to serve those vigilant servants who are faithful, and a time when God's pilgrim people are challenged to go forward with the faith of Abraham that God is able to bring forth life from death.

Praying with Scripture

- Ask Christ to help you find the true treasurers of your heart.

- Pray for Church leaders during a time of "testing."

- Think of the Sunday Eucharist as a time when Christ invites you to sit at table as he serves you.

The Assumption of the Blessed Virgin Mary

Readings: Rev 11:19; 12:1-6, 10; Ps 45; 1 Cor 15:20-27;
Luke 1:39-56

> **"My soul proclaims the greatness of the Lord"**
> **(Luke 1:46).**

Mary's Joy, Our Promise

A difficulty in reflecting or preaching on the Assumption has always been the absence of any biblical account that "the ever Virgin Mary, having completed the course of her earthly life, was assumed body and soul into heavenly glory" (Pope Pius XII, *Munificentissimus Deus,* [November 1, 1950] no. 44). The dogma arose from centuries of reflection on the relation of Mary to the total Christ-event. The readings today capture this. Paul looks to the transformation of all in Christ and to the resurrection of their bodies. Today's feast proclaims that Mary now lives with that complete transformation that is our hope.

The gospel, Mary's song, the *Magnificat,* is not only one of the most endearing and powerful parts of the Christian Bible, but it is a magnificent summary of the belief of the biblical people of Israel. Mary stands in the tradition of Miriam, who celebrates God's deliverance from Egypt by calling the community to "sing to the LORD, for he is gloriously triumphant" (Exod 15:21), and of Judith, who sings of God's salvation for the people (Jdt 16:1-17). Though abounding in allusions to the Old Testament and especially the psalms, Mary's song of praise most closely parallels that of Hannah, who rejoices at the gift of a son (1 Sam 2:1-11). Mary heralds with joy a God of reversals, who exalts a "lowly servant," whom all generations will now call blessed. She sings of God's mercy to the weak, of casting down the mighty from their thrones and lifting up the lowly. Mary's assumption is her ultimate "lifting up," as will be our resurrection.

In Luke, Mary is the one who hears God's word, acts upon it, and brings forth Christ to the world. From her body is formed the incarnate

Son of God, a symbol that the body of every Christian is a bearer of God's presence. When reflecting on the meeting between Elizabeth and Mary and on Mary's praise, St. Ambrose wrote: "Let Mary's soul be in each of you to proclaim the greatness of the Lord. Let her spirit be in each to rejoice in the Lord. Christ has only one mother in the flesh, but we all bring forth Christ in faith" (*Commentary on the Gospel of Luke,* 2.27). The themes for this feast are rich: a woman raised to the presence of God; a humble servant who is the agent of God's reversals; a model for us on our journey, from responding, "Let it be done," to ultimate transformation, when "the last enemy to be destroyed is death" (1 Cor 15:26).

PRAYING WITH SCRIPTURE

- Read prayerfully Mary's *Magnificat,* pausing with prayers of gratitude and petition to Mary.

- Pray over ways in which your life proclaims the greatness of God.

- Mary takes the side of the poor, the powerless, and the marginal. As "Mother of the Church," how does she challenge us today?

Twenty-First Sunday in Ordinary Time

Readings: Isa 66:18-21; Ps 117; Heb 12:5-7, 11-13; Luke 13:22-30

> **"I come to gather nations of every language;
> they shall come and see my glory" (Isa 66:18).**

THE CHURCH, A GATED COMMUNITY?

A number of years ago I was participating in an ecumenical dialogue in the then divided city of Berlin. At the dividing line were the remnants of the colossal Brandenburg Gate, through which Hitler's armies marched. On a visit to the Pergamon Museum of Antiquity in East Berlin, I sat before the monumental Babylonian Ishtar Gate, through which the Judean exiles were marched. Broad gates are for armies and characterize oppressive power. In today's gospel Jesus says that we must enter by the narrow gate. Narrow gates lead into gardens and humble homes; often we must even stoop to enter them. One enters narrow gates usually by invitation.

Jesus then shifts the metaphor to entry into a house, when people will knock and be refused admittance. He then goes on to challenge the whole concept of religious privilege. Those who will stand outside knocking are former table companions who listened to his teaching; they will be excluded (Matthew 7:21-23 identifies these as unfaithful Christian disciples). The "few" who are admitted recall the prophetic heritage; a remnant will return to God in repentance (e.g., Isa 1:18-20). They are called by Zephaniah a people humble and lowly who seek refuge in the Lord (3:12). Jesus also attacks those who lay exclusive claim to the heritage of Abraham and the prophets; rather, people will come from the four corners of the earth to eat in the kingdom of God, echoing Isaiah's vision of the eschatological banquet (Isa 25:6-8) and the command from the first reading to gather "nations of every language."

The gospel presents a paradox of exclusion and inclusion. Neither familiarity with Jesus nor membership in a chosen people assures admittance to the banquet, and yet Jesus includes a small remnant that enters by the narrow gate, perhaps bowed down and with stragglers in the procession (the "last who will be first"). This recalls both Mary's hymn that the lowly will be exalted and Simeon's prediction that "this child is destined for the fall and rise of many in Israel" (Luke 2:34), as well as Luke's concern that it is the marginal and suffering people of the world whom Jesus will welcome (Luke 4:16-30). Christians today overly concerned about impressive gates and religious identity may find some surprising table companions at the messianic banquet and should not wait to issue an invitation but rather say, "Just come in, not by the grand entrance, but by the little gate at the side of the church!"

PRAYING WITH SCRIPTURE

- Pray in gratitude for the peoples from the four corners of the earth who are joining our eucharistic banquets.

- In prayer, hear the challenge of the responsorial psalm: "Go out to all the world and tell the good news."

- What "narrow gates" must we enter in order to enjoy Christ's eucharistic banquet?

Twenty-Second Sunday in Ordinary Time

Readings: Sir 3:17-18, 20, 28-29; Ps 68; Heb 12:18-19, 22-24a;
Luke 14:1, 7-14

"God gives a home to the forsaken" (Ps 68:7a).

CHECK THE GUEST LIST!

More than any other evangelist, Luke portrays Jesus at meals. He eats not only with tax collectors and sinners, as in Mark and Matthew, but with friends such as Martha and Mary, and dines frequently with Pharisees. In antiquity meals were important community events, with various rituals governing social status and seating. (Every mother of the bride may appreciate this as she struggles with seating at the wedding reception.) Pharisees were especially noted for careful banquet rules, since they were concerned about purity and formed "eating clubs," where they could feel at home and reflect on the Scriptures.

Jesus shares a Sabbath meal with a "leading Pharisee," yet with an ominous note, since people are "keeping an eye on him." Unfortunately, by omitting 14:2-6, the Lectionary eviscerates the drama and meaning of the whole section. A man afflicted with dropsy appears, interrupting the banquet, much like the "sinful woman" in Luke 7:37. Jesus then asks the lawyers (scribes) and Pharisees if it is lawful to heal on the Sabbath—perhaps a topic discussed at their banquets. In the face of their silence, Jesus heals the man and then asks whether they would save a child who falls into a well on a Sabbath, and again receives no answer, even though Jewish law allowed life-saving activities on the Sabbath. Jesus views the man's debilitating illness as a living death.

Today's gospel picks up where Jesus expresses common wisdom about dining etiquette (see Prov 25:6-7; Sir 3:17-20). Rather than seeking places of honor, his listeners are advised to go to the lowest place to avoid the humiliation of being asked to move, with the chance that the host will notice their proper deference and invite them to a higher position. (Not seeking places in the front seems engraved in every Catholic's imagination as they huddle in the back of church.) Jesus' words seem like jejune advice from one who himself breaks social taboos and exhorts his followers to radical discipleship.

Then Jesus makes another turn. Echoing Mary's vision in the *Magnificat*, he again invokes the theme of reversal by stating that those who exalt themselves will be humbled, while the humble will be exalted, and goes on to shatter those very dining rituals that he seemed to support. Reciprocity and invitations to people of equal status were the twin pillars of ancient dining customs. Jesus rejects this principle and says, rather, you should invite "the poor, the crippled, the lame, the blind," groups of no status, who, Jesus notes, will not be able to pay you back. These groups are not simply economically poor and social outcasts but are often seen as unclean. The Qumran community celebrated their meals as an anticipation of the great eschatological banquet, but ineligible for participation were "the lame, the blind, and the crippled" (*War Scroll*, 7:4-6). Jesus, too, looks to the eschatological banquet at the resurrection of the righteous, which is symbolized in the present by the inclusion of these very outcasts.

Today no Christian church follows literally the advice of Jesus. Could you picture a fund-raising dinner without inviting friends, neighbors, or wealthy people who could reciprocate? Would every carefully selected guest table have a few stragglers from the street to spice up the conversation? The most authentic followers of Jesus' advice today are found in Catholic Worker soup kitchens or at places like Jonah House in Baltimore, where the late Philip Berrigan, his wife, Liz McAlister, and extended family welcomed poor and suffering people.

The meals of Jesus throughout Luke have eucharistic overtones, so his Gospel can suggest proper "etiquette" for our celebrations. Eating with Jesus should be a time of healing, which can shock even customary religious sensitivities. Liturgy should be inclusive of those whom our society today views as unworthy or unclean. Such invitations are the prelude to admittance to the banquet of the just (righteous) who humbled themselves by associating with those very people to whom Jesus announces the benefits of God's reign (Luke 4:16-19).

PRAYING WITH SCRIPTURE

- Pray over how the Sunday Eucharist may be a time of healing and of acceptance of others.

- The threat of starvation and malnutrition looms over vast parts of the human family. In prayer, ask how your parish or community can address this.

- Sirach says that "an attentive ear is the joy of the wise." What voices must we hear today?

Twenty-Third Sunday in Ordinary Time

Readings: Wis 9:13-18b; Ps 90; Phlm 9-10, 12-17; Luke 14:25-33

"Who can conceive what the LORD intends?" (Wis 9:13).

I NEVER PROMISED A ROSE GARDEN

Over the past weeks the readings alternate between presenting Jesus as a model of compassion and mercy and as a leader who makes harsh demands of his followers (for example, entering the narrow gate, casting fire on the earth, bringing division among families). In today's gospel the demands mount: one cannot be a disciple without hating family and even his or her own life. Most people would see Jesus' advice as downright destructive when family difficulties cause so much suffering today; it is also jarring in a Church which stresses that the family is the fundamental human community. Historically these statements may reflect an actual period when Christian discipleship did involve wrenching separation from loved ones and went against established social customs. Also the word "hate" has been widely interpreted, not as emotional anger or desire of harm to others, but as "loving less" when faced with a fundamental life choice (see Matt 10:37)—one that makes a disciple turn his or her own life upside down. For Jesus, this is equivalent to carrying one's cross.

Jesus then appends two parables that in effect say, "If you follow me, you better know what you are getting into and prepare for the long haul." These parables are, however, paradoxical. Both suggest that persons preparing for the future should take careful stock of whether they have resources necessary either to complete a construction project or to fight a war. But Jesus concludes, "In the same way, anyone of you who does not renounce all his possessions cannot be my disciple" (14:33). The main point of comparison is an accurate assessment of what the future demands. A future of following Jesus does not depend on material resources or on power (the king preparing for battle), but on complete trust in God. Luke has already warned against an initial joyful and enthusiastic response to Jesus' word that then withers and dies in time of trial (8:13). Proper discernment must precede radical discipleship.

These dramatic conditions for discipleship were scarcely observed throughout the early Church or by all Christians throughout history. They have often been misused as literal prescriptions for religious life, when, for example, religious could not visit dying family members. Is their relevance, then, only as memory of a utopian vision by Jesus the martyred prophet, or are they limited to a few heroic saints, even though Jesus says "anyone of you"? They are, rather, indicative of a kind of total commitment that every follower of Christ should be prepared to live. The radical demands of Jesus call on us to center our lives on the suffering and risen Christ, which relativizes even family values and the security of possessions. Yet the ultimate reversal remains that the one who chooses the kingdom of God over family will receive "an overabundant return in this present age and eternal life in the age to come" (Luke 18:30), and that those who seek to preserve their lives will lose them, while those who lose them will save them (Luke 17:33).

Praying with Scripture

- Thinking of the challenges you face, pray for the wisdom to find "the resources to finish" (Luke 14:30).

- Pray over how even family relationships and material needs may hinder a more intense following of Christ.

- Contrast the freedom that Jesus expects of his disciples with the overriding concern for security today.

Twenty-Fourth Sunday in Ordinary Time

Readings: Exod 32:7-11, 13-14; Ps 51; 1 Tim 1:12-17;
Luke 15:1-10 (15:1-32)

"Have mercy on me, O God, in your goodness"
(Ps 51:3).

LOOK IN LOST AND FOUND

The parables of Luke 15, often called "The Gospel within the Gospel," epitomize Luke's message of forgiveness and repentance. These motifs appear more frequently in Luke than in any other Gospel: Zechariah heralds the coming of the Lord who will bring forgiveness of sin (1:77), and both John and Jesus initiate their ministries by announcing forgiveness and repentance. Jesus' final commission to his disciples is to preach repentance and forgiveness to all nations (24:47), which is a recurring theme in the sermons of the Acts of the Apostles and which defines the life work of Paul (Acts 26:17-19).

Repentance evokes images of sorrow for offending God, turning away from sinful acts and returning to God, along with a "firm purpose of amendment." Biblical ideas of repentance are much richer. The Hebrew term *teshubah* evokes a return to God by a person who has already experienced God's "goodness and compassion" (Psalm 51), and the Greek, *metanoia*, suggests a "second look," "taking stock," "recollection and renewal." Such "repentance" leads to forgiveness (literally "sending away") of sin, with overtones of pardon, release from captivity, and cancellation of punishment.

In the Cycle C of the Lectionary, the story of the returning prodigal son appears also as the gospel for the Fourth Sunday of Lent, so today provides a fine opportunity to reflect on the two short preceding parables. These parables respond to criticism by certain Pharisees and scribes over Jesus' frequent practice of welcoming and eating with tax collectors and sinners. Jesus responds to his critics with a question: "What man among you having a hundred sheep . . . ?" asking them ironically to identify with a shepherd, which was one of the occupations disdained by strict religious observers. Irrationally, this shepherd leaves ninety-nine of his flock "in the desert" (where danger lurks and wild beasts roam) to search out one lost one, which he tenderly carries home on his shoulders. Then he summons his friends and neighbors and throws a party, which Jesus says reflects a heavenly party, where there will be "more joy in heaven over one sinner who repents than over ninety-nine righteous people who have no need of repentance."

The second parable of finding the lost coin challenges the leaders to move beyond their privileged position and to see the world through the eyes of a woman searching for a lost coin—perhaps part of her original dowry, which she kept in trust. This juxtaposition of a story of a woman and a man is a very familiar Lukan compositional technique (for example, the canticles of Mary and Zechariah; the raising of the widow's son, followed by the healing of the centurion's servant; the parable of the widow and the unjust judge). The woman's search is more intense; she lights a lamp, sweeps the house, and searches "carefully." After finding the coin, she calls together her friends and says, "Rejoice with me because I have found the coin that I lost." The celebration may have cost as much as the coin that was lost. Finding results in exuberant generosity.

The sayings of Jesus on repentance are in tension with the parables themselves. Repentance suggests return or conversion, but neither the wandering sheep nor the lost coin do anything except getting lost. The dramatic surprise in each comes from the seeking shepherd and the searching woman, which make us realize that repentance is much more being found by a searching God than anything that we do. Writing to Timothy, Paul expresses this beautifully: "I have been mercifully treated" and "the grace of our Lord has been abundant." A deep strain of Pelagian theology runs through religious consciousness in the United States, where effort and reward are so prized. These parables are decidedly "un-American." Repentance is not climbing a ladder of sorrow and regret toward God, but the joy of discovery by a searching God.

All three parables of Luke 15 end with a party or a celebration of finding. Today people, especially the young, often wander from the Church for myriad reasons, only to return later. The Church needs more rituals of finding when the joy of return can be celebrated. I remember a ceremony in the Oakland cathedral of reconciliation and acceptance of people who had been marginally Catholic. It was Holy Thursday. The returning Catholics processed up the aisle with looks of expectant joy. The bishop went through the rite of reconciliation, and after the homily he washed their feet. In front of me was an older couple, who wept with joy as they celebrated the finding of their lost daughter or son. This Maundy Thursday Eucharist was truly a celebration of finding as the joy in heaven spilled over on the earth.

The setting of these parables must also be highlighted. One of the most shocking of Jesus' actions was his penchant for associating with religious and social misfits, to the apparent neglect of the dutiful. Jesus practiced communion and companionship (literally "sharing bread") that lead to repentance, an experience of being found and accepted by a loving God. As José Combin wrote recently, while Jesus preached and practiced forgiveness of sin, too often the contemporary Church is overly concerned with prevention of sin. To find Christ today, skip home furnishing and check in lost and found.

PRAYING WITH SCRIPTURE

- Prayerfully reflect on how the image of the "foolish shepherd" and the searching woman challenge your image of God.

- Pray over those moments when, feeling lost, you experienced God's searching love.

- Pray over how families and Christian communities might create celebrations of "finding."

Twenty-Fifth Sunday in Ordinary Time

Readings: Amos 8:4-7; Ps 113; 1 Tim 2:1-8; Luke 16:1-13

"He raises up the lowly from the dust"(Ps 113:7).

BALANCING THE BOOKS!

As the bright light of summer yields to the soft hues of autumn, while students settle into school and parish activities move into high gear, Christians often ponder vacation expenses, tuition bills, and the impending cost of new projects. Life in Christ seems to be taken over by calculator and computer. Yet the theme of today's readings is that our salvation is deeply intertwined with how we engage the goods of this world.

Amos, as elsewhere in his sayings, thunders against those practices that foster the exploitation of the poor peasantry by expansionist policies of the rich upper classes (see Amos 2:6-8; 4:1-3); they violate sacred religious law to gain more time for dishonest practices that send people into slavery (5:7-15, 21-24). Yet today's story of the Unjust Steward, which is one of the most enigmatic parables of the Gospels, seems to condone the very kind of skullduggery that Amos rants against. There have been more explanations of this text than the one hundred measures of oil owed to the master.

We meet initially a steward (manager) of a wealthy person's land, roughly equivalent to a CEO of a large corporation. Some kind of audit reveals that he had been squandering the resources of the estate, and he is called on the carpet to explain himself. Realizing that no defense is possible, and aware that he may be sent to the mines ("dig") or become a street beggar, he devises a plan. By reducing the debts owed to his master, he hopes to curry favor with the debtors, so that they might hire him later. He calls them in one by one. One owes the equivalent of 1000 barrels of olive oil, which he immediately halves; and another, roughly 1100 bushels of wheat, which he reduces by 20 percent. Shockingly, the parable itself concludes with the simple statement, "the master commended that dishonest steward for acting prudently."

The first readers of this parable found it as shocking and enigmatic as we do today, since Luke 16:9-13 present a chain of sayings on wealth that scarcely explain the parable. While praising the shrewdness of the children of this world, Jesus tells his disciples to "make friends (for yourselves) with dishonest wealth" and praises actions that are the direct opposite of those of the manipulating manager: "The person who is trustworthy in very small matters is also trustworthy in great ones," and "No servant can serve two masters," which is exactly what the manger succeeds in doing.

The most common explanation of the parable is a "jesuitical" distinction that what Jesus praises is not the dishonesty of the manager but his prudence or shrewdness in a difficult time. Others stress the moral casuistry surrounding Jewish laws against lending money at interest. By letting the manager handle the loan terms, the owner can stay "out of the loop," while benefiting from exorbitant interest rates. When the manager juggles the books, he is simply reducing the profit he would have gained from the loans and restores to the manager the amount of the initial loan (perhaps with some profit included). Here the manager is an example of a person who, when faced with a critical situation (for instance, the demands of Jesus' teaching), will sacrifice his or her own gain to respond. A third set of explanations focuses on the parable as an instance of a common folk motif of a roguish but lovable inferior outwitting a demanding master.

Such attempts prove the potential for multiple meanings of biblical texts. Too often overlooked is the similarity between the parables of the Unjust Steward and the preceding Prodigal Son. Both parables portray a person facing a life-threatening situation because the central character has "squandered" resources—the son, his father's; the manager, his master's. Each person so caught utters a soliloquy and evolves a plan to extricate himself, with a rather self-serving motivation. In each case the hoped-for changed fortune will result in acceptance into a house, and in each case the narrative flow of the parable is determined by the figure of power (father, owner).

Most importantly, in both cases the plans of the wastrels are not realized but are transcended by the surprising action of first the father and then the rich man. Both people caught in a dilemma think in terms of reestablishing a proper order of justice or obligation, and both receive unexpected acceptance and are rescued from danger by what they receive, not by what they accomplish. This story might be called the parable of the Foolish Rich Man, who acts illogically, like the shepherd and the father of Luke 15, and thus evokes a world in which God does not exact punishment and cancels debts even in the midst of human machinations.

PRAYING WITH SCRIPTURE

- The first readings today and next Sunday are from Amos; read prayerfully the book of Amos and reflect on how his message challenges us today.

- Pray over ways in which we, as "rich Americans," might become "trustworthy in great matters."

- Pray over those times when God's forgiveness has surpassed your plans and expectations.

Twenty-Sixth Sunday in Ordinary Time

Readings: Amos 6:1a, 4-7; Ps 146; 1 Tim 6:11-16; Luke 16:19-31

> "The LORD gives sight to the blind.
> The LORD raises up those who were bowed down;
> the LORD loves the just" (Ps 146:8).

TIME FOR A VISION AND HEARING CHECK

I was thinking about today's readings while halfheartedly watching one of the morning TV news shows. There was a segment on the rising number of spas for dogs, where, with congenial companions, they could get a complete makeover—haircut, shampoo, pedicure—topped off by a dose of aroma therapy. Bring back Amos thundering against the complacent in Zion for their conspicuous consumption and regal living (writing music like David)! While pet spas may be a bit humorous, they are but a symptom of the growing and massive disparity of wealth in the United States, the richest country in the world with one of the highest rates of children living in poverty.

The gospel narrative of the rich man and poor Lazarus is the Lukan culmination of Jesus' teaching about the danger of wealth. Because the good news originates among the *'anawim*, marginal and humble people who are open to God—Zechariah, Mary, the shepherds, Anna and Simeon—Luke's Gospel is often called the "Gospel of the poor." Yet there is far more material about the dangers of great wealth and the pitfalls faced by the rich in responding to the good news, so the Gospel might rightly be called "Somber News for the Wealthy."

Today's gospel begins with a vivid contrast: designation of status (rich) vs. poor; dressed in purple garments of fine linen (both very costly in the ancient world) vs. being clothed in ulcerous sores; sumptuous daily meals, most likely with other rich dinner guests, vs. scavenging for food with dogs as his only companions. Yet the poor man's name (rare in parables), Lazarus (literally "God helps"), is a hint of the reversal of fate that will unfold.

The poor man dies and angels carry him to the bosom of Abraham, while the rich man dies but has a funeral (normally a sign of God's favor). The parable shifts dramatically with a surprising reversal of fate: the rich man is in torment in the netherworld, but he looks up, sees Lazarus with Abraham, and begs "Father Abraham" to send Lazarus with a drop of water to cool his torment. Abraham, as the guardian of the covenant fidelity of the people, assumes the role of teacher, disclosing to the rich man the dire fate that awaits him. The key to understanding this harsh punishment is that the rich man first *sees* the very Lazarus who lay at his gate when the chasm between them is eternally fixed. During his lifetime his wealth created a gulf that made him blind to the sufferings of the poor man; now he can gaze on him only when it is too late.

Having realized his sinfulness, the rich man then begs Abraham to send Lazarus to warn his brothers, who apparently lived the same lavish lifestyle. Abraham replies that they have the same opportunities he had, the law and the prophets, a reference to the injunctions of the Torah to care for the poor and the needy, and the warnings of the prophets, like those of Amos. Somewhat persistently, the rich man shows an even deeper blindness to God's revelation and asks instead for some startling event, such as the return of Lazarus from the dead, to convince them. Abraham again states that without listening to the law and the prophets, the brothers will not be converted even if someone should rise from the dead.

This parable offers rich resources for reflection today. Throughout the Bible the overriding evil of great wealth is that it so takes over a person's life that it makes him or her deaf to the teaching of Torah and blind to the sufferings of neighbors. Today, as many people zip along freeways from plush offices to gated communities, one wonders how they can ever see the poor at their gates. Pope John Paul II has constantly invoked this parable to challenge the rich nations of the world to see the impoverished peoples often at their very doorstep.

Also of great importance is the abiding validity of "the law and the prophets" to form Christian conscience. Christians today believe in the risen Jesus, and perhaps some in Luke's community felt that this was enough; they no longer had to take seriously the Jewish tradition of justice and compassion for the weak. Stress on the risen and reigning Christ can engender a neo-triumphalism that focuses on liturgical pomp, resplendent buildings, and insular discussions of Catholic identity. But the one risen from the dead who offers salvation to us today is the same Jesus who listened to the voice of Moses and the prophets and offered love and acceptance to the marginalized of his day, while uttering sober warnings to the proud and prosperous. Like the brothers of

Lazarus, if we cannot plumb the social message of the Jewish Scriptures, the words of the risen Jesus will fall on deaf ears.

PRAYING WITH SCRIPTURE

- Prayerfully ask the risen Christ to open your eyes to the sufferings of others.

- Read prayerfully the book of Amos, Deuteronomy 15, and Isaiah 1:1-20, while reflecting on how "the law and prophets" challenge you today.

- Recall how people like Lazarus have been a source of grace in your life.

Twenty-Seventh Sunday in Ordinary Time

Readings: Hab 1:2-3; 2:2-4; Ps 95; 2 Tim 1:6-8, 13-14; Luke 17:5-10

**"Bear your share of hardship for the gospel
with the strength that comes from God" (2 Tim 1:8).**

STRANGE WORKING CONDITIONS!

"Destruction and violence are before me; / there is strife, and clamorous discord" (how sadly current!); / "When you have done all you have been commanded, say, 'We are unprofitable servants; we have done what we were obliged to do.'" Habakkuk's cry and Jesus' words hardly seem like good news to a congregation assembled on an autumn Sunday morning to be nurtured by God's word and by the sacrament of joy and thanksgiving. Yet, hearing God's word and memorializing Christ's passion involve a straightforward confrontation with rampant evil and a sobering sense of the demands of discipleship.

The surprising and paradoxical quality of faith runs through the readings. In the face of destruction and suffering, Habakkuk is told that "the vision still has its time" and "presses on to fulfillment, and will not disappoint," and that the just person is one who will live because of faith. Faith here is not assenting to a series of doctrines but hope and steadfast expectation in the face of suffering and delay. The gospel gathers two of four somewhat unrelated sayings of Jesus (Luke 17:1-10—on scandal, forgiveness, faith, and service) that culminate with the request of the disciples, "Increase our faith." Rather than granting this, Jesus responds with the riddle that with faith even the size of a mustard seed (see Mark 4:31, "the smallest of all the seeds on the earth"), a person could command a mulberry (or sycamore) tree to blast off into the sea. Similar sayings in Matthew and Mark compare the power of such faith to the ability to cast mountains into the sea. While the disciples asked for a quantitative increase in faith, Jesus' example tells them of the quality of faith. Faith is not a collection of good deeds, but a quality of courage and love. *The Gospel of Thomas* has an interesting variation of this saying: "If two make peace with each other in this one house, they will say to the mountain, 'Move away,' and it will move away" (no. 48). In light of the horror and tragic events that constantly cut short so many innocent lives, peacemaking seems to be a miracle greater than trees flying into the sea.

The parable of the Unprofitable Servant seems both harsh and unrelated to the context, especially since earlier, in Luke 12:35-38, Jesus tells the story of a master who returns to find a faithful servant and seats him at table while he prepares the servant's meal. Today's parable is the reverse. A servant comes in from a long day of manual labor, and the master barks out, "Prepare something for me to eat," serve it to me, and you can have some when I am finished. Worse still is the application to the disciples: "So should it be with you. When you have done all you have been commanded," then count yourselves as unprofitable servants.

The readings today would be ideal to stress the value of faith over works. A person is made just, that is, put in right relation to God and neighbor, by faith and by hope in a vision that "presses on to fulfillment, and will not disappoint." Jesus' harsh parable warns against defining religion in terms of "doing all that is commanded." People often judge themselves and others by how they observe various and manifold rules. Doing all that is commanded can simply result in being unprofitable, that is, not really of any benefit to "the Lord."

Yet the warning against the unprofitable servant is prefaced by a promise that just a little bit of faith (the size of a mustard seed) can produce astounding results, while servile effort—doing just what is commanded—brings little benefit. Such faith involves keeping the vision alive. For some this may be a hope for a world in which justice and peace replace the violence and destruction so recently experienced and paraded constantly before our eyes. For others the vision involves respect for life in all its forms and at all stages; while for still others it is the vision of a renewed Church which, like the mustard seed, was planted at Vatican II. Those who wait in faithful trust and nurture the vision, even without doing all that is commanded, may in the end be like the earlier servant of Luke 12, whom the master feeds and serves. We call this our eucharistic gathering.

PRAYING WITH SCRIPTURE

- Like Habakkuk, write down your visions and pray in faith for their fulfillment.

- In prayer, honestly assess how often your faith involves concern about doing all that is commanded.

- Pray that God will work a miracle of bringing peace to divided nations and houses throughout the world.

Twenty-Eighth Sunday in Ordinary Time

Readings: 2 Kgs 5:14-17; Ps 98; 2 Tim 2:8-13; Luke 17:11-19

**"Has none but this foreigner returned
to give thanks to God?" (Luke 17:18).**

HOPE AMID THE RUINS

Karl Barth, one of the great theologians of the past century, urged people to read the Bible with a copy of the daily newspaper at their side. He realized that the Bible could challenge the way we view human life. I write these lines three days after the horrendous tragedy that washed over so many human lives when airliners were turned into missiles and flying coffins on September 11, 2001. Like many, I move between shocked disbelief as the same pictures roll by hour after hour, and deep sadness and sympathy, while trying to stifle thoughts of anger and revenge.

This Sunday's gospel delivers a message that many of us find difficult to absorb. On first reading it is a story of Jesus healing ten people from a physically devastating and socially isolating disease, along with an example of a single one who returned to give thanks to God, in contrast to the other nine. Yet the shock of the story, which drastically enriches its power, is the simple phrase that the one who returned "was a Samaritan."

At the time of Jesus, bitter hatred had long existed between Jews and Samaritans, even though they shared the Torah and venerated Moses. Like most deep-seated hatreds, the origin of the differences had long been buried under almost four centuries of violence and resentment. While recognizing the Pentateuch and revering Moses, the Samaritans rejected the royal Davidic ideology and resisted the rebuilding of the temple after the Babylonian Exile. Their place of worship was not Jerusalem but Mount Gerizim, where their temple had been burned by the Jewish high priest John Hyrcanus in 128 B.C. Shortly before the time of Jesus' ministry, at Passover, some Samaritans entered the Jewish temple secretly and scattered human bones there, forcing the cancellation of temple service and precipitating strict security around the temple (Josephus, *Jewish Antiquities*, 18.29). Later, Samaritans killed some Galileans who were making a festive pilgrimage to Jerusalem. In reprisal, the Jews enlisted a certain Eleazar, a notorious bandit chieftain, to burn Samaritan villages. The Gospel of John reflects this hatred in the surprise of the Samaritan woman that Jesus would ask her for a drink of water (John 4:9), and the charge by Jesus' opponents that he is "a Samaritan and [demon] possessed" (John 8:48).

The great shock of the narrative, then, is that the one who returns "glorifying God in a loud voice" and who gives thanks to God is a Samaritan whom Jesus calls "a foreigner" (the Greek literally means a person of a different kind or nature). This positive view of the Samaritan should be joined with the other major Samaritan incident, the parable of the Good Samaritan. These two Samaritan stories provide an arch from the initial stages of Jesus' long journey to Jerusalem to near its conclusion. Taken together, the two narratives provide exemplars of the greatest commandments: to love God with one's whole heart and soul and to love one's neighbor as one's self, and to glorify God by praise and thanksgiving (Luke 17:15, 18). The hated foreigners and outsiders become models for Jesus' Jewish hearers of the deepest meaning of God's revelation. The story also breaks through deep-seated images of the enemy and fosters respect and forgiveness.

Among the tragic victims of the destruction of United Flight 93 on September 11, 2001, was Deora Bodley, a junior at Santa Clara University. When Father Paul Locatelli, S.J., the president of the university, talked with her parents, they replied that "Deora and they would want peace among people and an earth that reflects harmony among all people, not recrimination or revenge." Such sentiments echo another person who died by violence in the prime of life: "Love your enemies, do good to those who hate you, bless those who curse you" (Luke 6:27-28).

The gospel cautions us today, even in the face of the recent horror, against characterizing people of another race or religion as enemies. This is no message of the "cheap grace" of easy forgiveness. In the story itself, both Jew and Samaritan are healed of an illness that isolates them from the human family. Only after being healed does the Samaritan leper return to give thanks and praise. The reconciling ministry of the Church today does not require blindness to the evil that infects humanity, but commitment to a long-term mission to free ourselves and those who would harm us from deep-seated hatreds and prejudice. The day after the heartbreaking events of September 11, there opened in Sarajevo the international conference, "Christians and Muslims in Europe: Responsibility and Religious Commitment in a Pluralised Society," with representatives of the leadership bodies of Catholics, Protestants, and Muslims. As September 11, 2001, sears our memories, we can only hope and pray constantly that September 12 will provide healing balm.

PRAYING WITH SCRIPTURE

- Pray in quiet gratitude for a particular gift of healing that you have received.

- Compose for yourself a prayer of reconciliation and forgiveness that is appropriate for our time.

- In prayer, recall "outsiders" who have given thanks and glory to God.

Twenty-Ninth Sunday in Ordinary Time

Readings: Exod 17:8-13; Ps 121; 2 Tim 3:14–4:2; Luke 18:1-8

"Pray always without becoming weary" (Luke 18:1).

THE WIDOW'S MIGHT

A friend once told me a story of a conversation with a rabbi who said that the New Testament was not a holy book. After he proposed a few sympathetic stabs at understanding the rabbi's statement, by admitting the more anti-Jewish sections of Matthew or Paul's view that Christ was the end of the law, the rabbi responded that he could understand these things in the first-century context, but the real problem is that the New Testament has no humor in it! Today's gospel, while continuing the theme of faithful and trusting prayer that echoes throughout the readings, contains a bit of saving humor.

The parable of the Widow and the Judge grew a bit like Topsy, with three different applications: an initial interpretation that it illustrates tireless prayer; a conclusion that justice will be done for God's faithful ones; and a final question of whether such faith will last. As often in Luke, the parable begins with a stark contrast between a heartless judge and a stalwart widow. As one who neither fears God nor respects any human being, the judge is in direct contrast to the ideal judge of 2 Chronicles 19:5-6, upon whom the fear of the Lord rests, while the prophets castigate venal and heartless judges (see Amos 2:6-7; 5:10-13).

The heart of the parable is the battle between the widow and the judge. In both the Old and New Testaments, the widow is a sad instance of powerlessness, often the victim of injustice (as frequently in many parts of our world). We should not think of the widow as aged and infirm, since the average life span was forty, and the parable itself portrays the widow as vigorous. She comes alone to the gate where the judge presides and does not take "no" for an answer. She seeks the justice denied her by some antagonist (perhaps an unwillingness by a relative of her late husband to return her dowry), and the judge refuses somewhat humorously, unabashedly glorying in his own lack of fear of God or humans.

Current translations mask the humor of the parable. During his soliloquy the judge says, "Because this widow keeps bothering me, I shall deliver a just decision for her lest she finally come and strike me" ("bother" in Greek literally means "causes me toil or labor" and is roughly equivalent to "work me over"). Most startling is the original of "come and strike me" (the original Greek, *hypōpiazō*, is a metaphor from ancient boxing and means "strike below the eye"). A modern paraphrase of the judge's reflections would be: "Because this widow is working me over, I will recognize her rights so she doesn't give me a black eye by her unwillingness to give up." The humor is that a woman fighting for her rights pummels a complacent and fearless judge like a faltering boxer. Jesus' hearers are confronted with a new vision of reality inaugurated by God's reign, where victims claim their rights and seek justice—often in a surprising and unsettling manner.

The following application of the parable is that God's justice is very different from human justice. God's justice is on the side of the weak and the vulnerable. God will secure it as the people cry out day and night. The concluding question about whether the Son of Man will find faith at his return is a Lukan adaptation to his community, who are aware of the delay of the return of Jesus and undergoing trial or testing (see Luke 11:4). Only through prayer can fidelity (faith) be assured. The continual prayer urged in the parable is not simply passive waiting but the active quest for justice.

Today more than ever the Church must be nurtured by the kind of prayer embodied by the woman—persistent and courageous prayer in the face of brutal evil. Like Moses praying for his beleaguered people, such prayer calls for the support of others. At times we can raise our arms in prayer only when others are holding them up as we grow weary. Yet not even this is enough. The psalm tells us that our help is from "the Lord, who made heaven and earth" and who, like Aaron with Moses, is "at your right hand."

PRAYING WITH SCRIPTURE

- Think of women who have been models of persistent and faithful prayer: Dorothy Day, Sojourner Truth, Teresa of Avila, and Mother Teresa.

- Pray over the ways in which you might hold up the arms of friends as they struggle to pray in difficult times.

- Thinking of powerless people in our society, pray that "God [will] secure the rights of his chosen ones."

Thirtieth Sunday in Ordinary Time

Readings: Sir 35:12-14, 16-18; Ps 34; 2 Tim 4:6-8, 16-18;
Luke 18:9-14

"The prayer of the lowly pierces the clouds" (Sir 35:17).

TRIAL BY PRAYER

Today's gospel concludes a diptych on prayer begun last Sunday in the familiar Lukan pattern of juxtaposing a story in which a woman is a central character, with another character, a male protagonist. It also provides a bridge to next Sunday, when another tax collector is praised.

The beginning of the parable seems harsh: Jesus speaks to people who are convinced of their own righteous state before God and despise everyone else. (Since the previous parable spoke of God's chosen ones, this rebuke may have in mind Christian disciples.) Contemporary Christians, however, hear this parable with a strong bias against the Pharisee. The Pharisees were part of the many Jewish reform movements in the first century; they were lay, not priestly, and sought to find God's presence in all the daily routines of life. It is not surprising that a Pharisee goes to the temple to pray, and even his prayer is not as self-serving as it seems. The original hearers would not have been instantly critical. His prayer is twofold: a prayer of thanksgiving (*eucharistō*) to God for preservation from sin and an account of his fidelity in observing the prescribed fast and in giving tithes. Even the converted Pharisee Paul can boast of his piety and observance of the law and contrast his practices to those of others (Phil 3:4-6), and in one of the psalms from Qumran we hear, "I praise you, O Lord, that you have not allowed my lot to fall among the worthless community" (*Hodayot*, 7:34). To thank God for election and to speak of one's devotion do not of themselves make a prayer hypocritical or self-congratulatory.

What is surprising is the presence of the tax collector. These are not the "publicans" mentioned in the classical sources, that is, powerful people who gained the contract to collect taxes and engaged in massive exploitation, so much so that Julius Caesar suppressed the institution. Instead, they are rather petty bureaucrats who collected taxes for the ruling Romans or Herodian kings. They were disliked as agents of oppressive regimes, probably did engage in shady transactions, and were also thought to be unclean because of frequent contact with Gentiles at forbidden times. Throughout the Gospel Jesus betrays a penchant for associating with them, so much so that before he is ever called Lord and Christ, his title seems to be "glutton and drunkard, a friend of tax collectors and sinners" (Luke 7:34).

The defect of the Pharisee is not that he gives thanks for what God has done for him (protecting him from evildoers), but that he harbors prideful disdain for other people. He contrasts himself with a rash of unsavory people—greedy, dishonest, adulterous—but saves the tax collector for the end. His very position of prayer betrays his pride. He steps apart from the crowd as if God could not notice him wherever he is. The tax collector simply stands at a distance and will not even raise his eyes to heaven. His bodily gesture is itself a prayer before he pleads, "O God, be merciful to me a sinner!" He goes home made just in God's eyes. The justice of God accepts the unjust and the ungodly (see Rom 5:6-8) and is harsh on the dutiful and the respectable. The parable summons us to a prayer of love and trust in God's mercy and frees us of the need to tell God who is a sinner and who is not.

PRAYING WITH SCRIPTURE

- In confidence pray often the prayer of the tax collector, "God, be merciful to me a sinner."

- Prayerfully examine those tendencies to define your goodness in contrast to the defects of others.

- The psalmist proclaims that "the LORD is close to the brokenhearted." Repeat this quietly during times of trial.

Thirty-First Sunday in Ordinary Time

Readings: Wis 11:22–12:2; Ps 145; 2 Thess 1:11–2:2; Luke 19:1-10

**"The Lord is gracious and merciful,
slow to anger and of great kindness" (Ps 145:8).**

Hope for the Upwardly Mobile

In his wonderful novel *Handling Sin,* Michael Malone portrays Raleigh Whittier Hayes, a somewhat proper lawyer in a small Southern town, whose life begins to fall apart when his eccentric father, a defrocked Episcopalian priest, flees from a hospital bed with a young prostitute. Hayes "did believe in God, but, frankly he didn't trust him, and saw no reason in the world why he should. If God's idea of salvation was Jesus Christ, God was too eccentric to rely on." Hayes had read the New Testament, but "in his personal opinion Christ's advice sounded like civic sabotage, moral lunacy, social anarchy, and business disaster. Hayes had been a serious young man; and he still believed in virtue, which he suspected Christ of ridiculing by gleefully making up stories in which decent people were cheated by wastrels and the deserving blithely passed over in favor of bums." One of the passages that must have disturbed Hayes was today's gospel.

In Luke, the story of Zacchaeus, the chief tax collector (roughly equivalent to a district director of the IRS), occurs near the conclusion of Jesus' journey to Jerusalem, where he teaches his disciples the virtues and values they are to have as they move outward *from* Jerusalem (Acts 1:8). This incident also follows closely the story of the rich ruler whose wealth keeps him from following Jesus, while here salvation comes to "a wealthy man."

Luke's narrative contains both pathos and humor. Zacchaeus wants to see Jesus, but his position and wealth carry little clout, because the crowd will not even clear away to give him a look—he is also a victim of "sizeism." Breaking all cultural taboos, he runs ahead of the crowd and scampers up a sycamore tree—most likely accompanied by hoots and jeers—and positions himself where he can see Jesus. Neither wealth nor social status kept Zacchaeus from being scorned as an outsider by the religiously proper. Before he utters a word, Jesus looks up and simply says, "Come down quickly, for today I must stay at your house." Zacchaeus jumps out of the tree, goes home, and happily receives Jesus. The language here reflects the frequent Lukan theme of the joy that Jesus will bring. Remember Mary's words, "My spirit rejoices in God my savior" (Luke 1:47), and the message of great joy to the shepherds (Luke 2:10), as well as the importance of hospitality. Not everyone shares the joy, since the crowd begins to "grumble," the same term and the same complaint voiced by the scribes and Pharisees when Jesus eats with tax collectors and sinners and tells parables of losing and finding (Luke 15:1).

In contrast to the crowd's description of his house as that of a sinner, Zacchaeus proclaims his fidelity to God's law and shows that his wealth is not an obstacle to salvation. He gives half of his possessions to the poor. Such generosity reflects Tobit 4:10-11: "Almsgiving frees one from death, and . . . alms are a worthy offering in the sight of the Most High." If he has extorted money (which tax collectors were wont to do), he restores it fourfold. Fourfold restitution is demanded in Exodus 21:37 and was also known in Roman law. Jesus then pronounces that salvation has come to this house "today" and calls Zacchaeus a son of Abraham. Though classed as a sinner and socially marginal, he is really one who follows the Jewish laws on almsgiving and restitution. In ironic remembrance of the rich man who cries out from Hades to Abraham as father, only to have his prayer rejected because his wealth blinded him to the needs of the poor, Zacchaeus is a true child of Abraham by using his wealth in service of justice and charity.

This short narrative is a treasure trove of Lukan themes. Though Zacchaeus wants to see Jesus, it is Jesus who first sees him and calls him, as he summons disciples throughout the Gospel. In seeking to find Jesus, we are often found by him. Jesus' self-identity is as one who came to seek and save the lost, those bums and wastrels that so annoyed Raleigh Whittier Hayes. The lost Zacchaeus is found because he rises above the crowd and risks ridicule.

Christians must reflect on the price of rote conformity and unwillingness to buck current wisdom and values. Yet, as in the parables of Luke 15, finding is celebrated. Jesus becomes a guest and brings joy to the house. Zacchaeus is praised, not for practicing any particular "Christian" virtue (he never affirms faith in Jesus), but because of his fidelity to the covenant with Abraham and his fidelity to the Jewish laws. The Jewish faith and its Scriptures remain a covenant never revoked for Christians today. This story also offers good news to the wealthy today. If they welcome Jesus to their house with joy and do works of justice and charity, then salvation will come to their houses.

PRAYING WITH SCRIPTURE

- Pray over how you would welcome Jesus to your home.
- Discover your "inner" Raleigh Whittier Hayes as you wonder about the Church's concern for the marginal today.
- In prayer, reflect on how your gifts may benefit others.

Thirty-Second Sunday in Ordinary Time

Readings: 2 Macc 7:1-2, 9-14; Ps 17; 2 Thess 2:16–3:5;
Luke 20:27-38

> **"May the Lord direct your hearts to the love of God**
> **and to the endurance of Christ"(2 Thess 3:5).**

Where, Death, Is Your Victory?

As the liturgical year winds down, the gospels for the next four weeks address our deepest fears and offer our most profound hope. Today Jesus speaks of God as a God of the living who promises that the ones who will rise will be God's children. Next week the readings speak of the persecutions that will precede the return of the Son of Man, with the promise to Jesus' disciples that "not a hair on your head will be destroyed." The feast of Christ the King shows Jesus offering salvation and paradise at the moment of his death, and the First Sunday of Advent turns again to preparation for the return of the Son of Man.

These Sundays evoked a profound pathos in the autumn of 2001 after the attacks of September 11, 2001, when violence, death, and destruction were followed by rituals of mourning and grief. But a thread winding through this tapestry of readings is the victory over death and the promise of unending life. In the gospel today, the Sadducees, who accepted the authority of the Torah alone and did not believe in the resurrection, try to trap Jesus over the meaning of Scripture. They quote the so-called law of Levirate marriage from Deuteronomy 25:5, which says that if a man's brother dies, his widow must marry the surviving brother, and the first-born son is to continue the name and line of the deceased brother. Apparently knowing of Jesus' belief in the resurrection (which he shared with the Pharisees), they offer an absurd interpretation: seven brothers for one bride, and they crassly ask whose wife she shall be at the resurrection. Adept at Scripture himself, Jesus contrasts their understanding with a true understanding of resurrection and cites one of the most important texts for all Jews, the revelation of God to Moses that God is a God of the living, not of the dead. Jesus in effect says that true interpretation of Scripture depends on having the proper perspective on the nature of God.

Important in this gospel is the contrast between "the children of this age" and "the children of God . . . who will rise" (literally, "the sons of the resurrection who are sons of God"). Throughout Luke the children of this age are concerned about status honor, relationships of debt, and reciprocity (see 16:8), while children of God are those marked by mercy, generosity, and love of enemies. When Jesus says that the children of this age neither marry nor are given in marriage, he is not advocating universal celibacy but counters the materialistic and pragmatic view of the Sadducees that the wife is handed from brother to brother to assure male honor.

This gospel and those for the coming weeks then affirm the victory of God and God's love over the power of death. This victory evokes the dramatic first reading featuring the excerpt from the martyrdom of the seven brothers during the persecution of Antiochus IV Epiphanes (175–164 B.C.) before the Maccabean revolt. Each of the brothers, urged on by their mother ("Mother Courage"), affirms their fidelity in the law and trust in the resurrection before unspeakable torture and death. The fourth brother shouts out in faith, "It is my choice to die at the hands of men with the God-given hope of being restored to life by him" (2 Macc 7:14) [NAB]. The fidelity and victory of the Maccabean martyrs are recalled by our Jewish brothers and sisters at the feast of Hanukkah, also celebrated at this time of the year.

Though so many people now are bowed over in grief and the faith of countless others is shaken by the specter of brutal and senseless violence, these seasonal readings offer hope. Separated spouses will live together as sons and daughters of the resurrection. Fidelity and trust in God form a hope stronger than brutal power, whether it be in 165 B.C. or 2001 A.D. The readings also summon us to live as sons or daughters of God and of the resurrection, people who can follow the way of Jesus as it has unfolded throughout the readings from Luke this past year. It is a way that ends for Jesus on the cross promising paradise, and a way that continues with us as the risen Jesus opens up the Scriptures and breaks bread and as we, like the pilgrims on the way to Emmaus, sorrowfully walk from the place of death and suffering.

PRAYING WITH SCRIPTURE

- On Veterans Day (November 11), pray in gratitude for those men and women who have sought peace and justice in a violent world and made the ultimate sacrifice.

- Pray continually for peace and for those suffering from war here and in other parts of the world.

- Compose expressions of faith in a God of the living who is more powerful than death.

Thirty-Third Sunday in Ordinary Time

Readings: Mal 3:19-20a; Ps 98; 2 Thess 3:7-12; Luke 21:5-19

"By your perseverance you will secure your lives"
(Luke 21:19).

FUTURE SHOCK

The readings today leave most Catholics ill at ease and puzzled, and they often relegate their message to fundamentalist TV evangelists shouting about the coming end of the world. Malachi thought that the day of the Lord was coming, and it didn't come; Jesus says that "this generation will not pass away" until all the predictions about the return of the Son of Man will be fulfilled (Luke 21:32), and Paul expected to be alive at the return of Jesus. And yet all these expectations were not fulfilled, and even the most ardent millennialists today are constantly revising their timetable. Though surfacing at times throughout history, a sense that the world is about to end, followed by the return of Jesus, has never been part of the mainstream of Catholic thought. We live between the times, not in anticipation of the end of time. T. S. Eliot may better express our consciousness: "This is the way the world ends / Not with a bang but a whimper" (*The Hollow Men*).

Of all the evangelists, Luke grapples most with the tradition of the imminent Second Coming. As this expectation begins to wane, Luke adapts older tradition to a growing sense that discipleship will be played out over the long course of history—somewhat awkwardly, since the proverb that not a hair on your head will be harmed follows a prediction of execution! He tells Christians to take up their cross daily (9:23) while they pray for their daily bread, every day (11:3). In today's gospel Luke's Jesus shifts the focus to the need for faithful witness and assures the disciples of God's protection in times of persecution. In Luke (as in John), the Spirit will guide the Church during the time of Jesus' absence. Jesus remembered and Jesus present, rather than Jesus expected, shapes their communities.

Jesus' predictions of the destruction of the temple, war, and natural disaster—all bringing persecution in their wake—seem hauntingly contemporary. Such language, called "apocalyptic" (= revelation of God's plan for history), flourished in the Bible in times of national crisis and often among persecuted people. Its purpose was not to foster speculation about *when* God would intervene, but to encourage dispirited people by proclaiming that God is in control of history and that punishment of the wicked will be God's doing, not that of human vengeance. This literature provides an alternate view of history, from God's side, and summons people to faith and hope.

Coming at the end of the "roaring nineties," the events of September 11, 2001, and the following weeks darkened the bright skies with threatening thunderclouds. A culture of fear pervaded even preschool classes, heightened by round-the-clock media saturation. Though Jesus speaks of suffering still in the future, Luke's community had already experienced the destruction of the temple, the death of the first apostles, and even betrayal by loved ones. Yet Luke's Jesus promises them words and a "wisdom" to sustain them, and says that their perseverance will save them.

As Luke gave words and wisdom to his community, the Church is summoned at this critical time to find words of hope for the future and a wisdom that will guide our lives. During his long pontificate, Pope John Paul II has constantly repeated two themes: "Do not fear" and the need for peace based on justice and concern for suffering people. Today's psalm response yearns for a God who will govern the world with justice and equity. As a community that embraces all people and all cultures, the Church possesses the unique ability to hear the voices of suffering in all languages and to see the image of God in people of every creed and color. Human suffering and even human sin can also offer a *kairos*, a privileged time for renewal, reflection, and new directions that may give birth to the hope that "there will arise / the sun of justice with its healing rays" (Mal 3:20).

PRAYING WITH SCRIPTURE

- Prayerfully place before God your fears and hopes about the future.

- Join with others in praying for "words and wisdom" that can guide a Church concerned about injustice and suffering.

- As the liturgical year draws to a close, pray with special gratitude for graces received over the past year.

The Solemnity of
Our Lord Jesus Christ the King

Readings: 2 Sam 5:1-3; Ps 122; Col 1:12-20; Luke 23:35-43

> **"Jesus, remember me when you come
> into your kingdom" (Luke 23:42).**

FIT FOR A KING

Ask a group of "boomers" what pops into their minds when they hear the word "king." Some candidates might be simply "The King" (Elvis) or the King of Pop, or more soberly some might remember "The Boss" singing, "Poor man wanna be rich / Rich man wanna be king / And a king ain't satisfied / Till he rules everything." The word "king" suggests someone at the top exercising power and receiving adulation from all quarters.

The first reading depicts the origin of the Davidic dynasty when David is anointed to shepherd and command the people of Israel. The king was God's vice-regent on earth, and Psalm 72 offers an idealized job description for the king. He is to "govern your people with justice," "he shall defend the afflicted among the people" and "save the children of the poor" [author's translation]. Though rarely realized in practice, this mandate was part of the continuing hope for a messianic, royal figure of the Davidic line.

The gospel on this feast of the Messiah-King Jesus turns the royal ideology on its head. He reigns not from a throne but from the gibbet of the cross. God who was to be the protector and bulwark of the king seems to have abandoned him as he faces a cursed death (Deut 27:26). Like the servant of Isaiah 53:3, he is despised and rejected as the bystanders ridicule the image of the saving king, challenging him to prove his kingship by coming down from the cross and thus betray his command to his disciples to take up their cross and follow him.

As the last selection from Luke in Cycle C, the crucifixion is an epitome of Lukan themes. Announced to the shepherds as savior, Jesus does this from the throne of the cross. The "good thief" (actually in Luke simply a "criminal") calls him simply Jesus, a gesture of intimacy but also the promised name given at birth for one who would reign as king (Luke 2:31-33). The criminal asks to be remembered by Jesus but receives much more—intimacy with him in paradise. Jesus, who took on the mantle of Isaiah to proclaim salvation to the poor and the marginal (4:18) and who came "to seek and to save what was lost" (19:10), promises salvation to one like himself, marginal and rejected. Luke's Jesus preaches reconciliation and love of enemies, and as he is led to execution, he heals the ear of the hostile high priest's servant, breaks down the hatred between Pilate and Herod, and dies with a prayer to his Father for the forgiveness of his executioners (23:34).

The salvation of the "good thief," later named Dismas in Christian thought, reminds me of those heroic people who have tried to bring hope and saving concern to criminals in our society. I remember especially Father Jack Hickey, O.P., a dynamic and charismatic chaplain at Vanderbilt University. Despite reservations from many quarters, but with help from dedicated lay partners, he founded "Dismas House." Unlike the setup of other Dismas houses, recent parolees lived and worked with college students in the hope that mutual understanding and healing would take place. In the last years of his life, Jack fought virulent cancer and exercised his "royal priesthood" from his personal cross. Since his all-too-early death from cancer in January 1987, the movement has blossomed into ten such houses.

Our lives are filled with such horrible instances of the abuse of power that royal imagery seems best retired. The reign of Jesus from the cross is a different vision of power. Paul tells us that now we are brought into the "kingdom of [God's] beloved Son," who reconciled "all things for him, / making peace by the blood of his cross / [through him], whether those on earth or those in heaven" (Col 1:20). Yet Jesus as king "ain't satisfied till he rules everything," but his rule is seeking the lost, offering salvation to those who call out to him, and making friends of enemies. Today Jesus' rule is our task.

Praying with Scripture

- Pray over words of forgiveness that you have heard from Jesus on the cross.

- Pray over ways in which your parish or religious community might show God's love to those called "criminals" today.

- Turn to Christ on the cross and pray for wisdom and courage in face of the call for peace and reconciliation.

Select Annotated Bibliography on Luke

Craddock, F. B. *Luke*. Interpretation: A Bible Commentary for Teaching and Preaching. Louisville, Ky.: Westminster/John Knox, 1990.

Fitzmyer, J. A. *The Gospel According to Luke, I–IX* and *The Gospel According to Luke, X–XXIV*. Anchor Bible 28 and 28A. Garden City, N.Y.: Doubleday, 1981, 1985. The best commentary in any language on Luke. The introductory essay, "A Sketch of Lukan Theology," in *Luke I–IX*, pp. 143–270, is the finest synthesis available of Luke's theology.

Green, Joel B. *The Gospel of Luke*. Grand Rapids, Mich.: Wm. B. Eerdmans, 1997. A scholarly commentary with excellent pastoral insights.

_____. *The Theology of the Gospel According to Luke*. New York: Cambridge University Press, 1995. Excellent, up-to-date overview of Luke's theology.

Hendrickx, Herman. *The Third Gospel for the Third World*. A Michael Glazier Book. Collegeville, Minn.: The Liturgical Press, 1997–2002. Multivolume work. Hendrickx taught for four decades in Manila. His works draw on this experience while containing great insights for all who read Luke.

Johnson, Luke T. *The Gospel of Luke*. Sacra Pagina 3. A Michael Glazier Book. Collegeville, Minn.: The Liturgical Press, 1991. Very interesting commentary written at a level for the "religious professional."

Karris, Robert J. "The Gospel According to Luke." In *The New Jerome Biblical Commentary*. Ed. Raymond E. Brown, Joseph A. Fitzmyer, and Roland E. Murphy. Englewood Cliffs, N.J.: Doubleday, 1990. Pp. 675–721.

Kodell, Jerome. *The Gospel According to Luke*. The Collegeville Bible Commentary 3. Collegeville, Minn.: The Liturgical Press, 1983. Part of a series that remains outstanding for personal and group study of the Bible. All the New Testament volumes are available also in the one-volume *Collegeville Bible Commentary—New Testament*, edited by Robert J. Karris, O.F.M. Collegeville, Minn.: The Liturgical Press, 1997.

LaVerdiere, Eugene. *Luke*. New Testament Message. A Michael Glazier Book. Collegeville, Minn.: The Liturgical Press, 1980.

Navone, J. *Themes of St. Luke*. Rome: Gregorian University, 1970. Available from Loyola University Press, Chicago. Excellent catalog of Lukan themes.

Powell, M. A. *What Are They Saying About Luke?* New York/Mahwah, N.J.: Paulist Press, 1989. Excellent synthesis and survey with an eleven-page annotated bibliography.

Reid, Barbara E. *Choosing the Better Part? Women in the Gospel of Luke.* College-ville, Minn.: The Liturgical Press, 1996.

_____. *Parables for Preachers: Year C, The Gospel of Luke.* Collegeville, Minn.: The Liturgical Press, 1999. Luke's distinctive theology appears strongly in the parables. Reid offers helpful exegesis and original insights.

Talbert, Charles. *Reading Luke: A Literary and Theological Commentary on the Third Gospel.* Macon, Ga.: Smyth & Helwys, 2002. Insightful commentary by a scholar who has worked three decades on Luke.

Tannehill, Robert. *Luke.* Abingdon New Testament Commentary. Nashville: Abingdon Press, 1996. Tannehill is one of the leading commentators on Luke, with a good pastoral sense.